CULTIVATE
YOUR
PERSONALITY

LISTENING TO THE HOLY SPIRIT
THROUGH THE ENNEAGRAM

BEVERLY KIMBALL

wesleyan
PUBLISHING HOUSE
wphstore.com
Fishers, IN

Copyright © 2023 by Beverly Kimball
Published by Wesleyan Publishing House, Fishers, Indiana 46037
www.wesleyan.org/wph
Printed in the United States of America
ISBN: 978-1-63257-516-6
ISBN (e-book): 978-1-63257-517-3

Names: Kimball, Beverly, 1969- author.
Title: Cultivate your personality : listening to the Holy Spirit through
  the Enneagram / by Beverly Kimball.
Description: Fishers, Indiana : Wesleyan Publishing House, 2023. | Includes
  bibliographical references. | Summary: "The Enneagram helps a person
  understand how God's Word and the Holy Spirit's power can bring about
  change in their life. People need to hear how seeking the Holy Spirit
  and the will of God in their life requires an internal look. Learning
  how we are uniquely created and how God uses those gifts and natural
  instincts to help others in the world is what most Christians are
  looking for. I believe this book will open up a journey for believers to
  discover how to become more like Christ through looking at how they are
  created"-- Provided by publisher.
Identifiers: LCCN 2022045686 | ISBN 9781632575166 (paperback) | ISBN
  9781632575173 (ebook)
Subjects: LCSH: Personality--Religious aspects--Christianity. | Enneagram.
Classification: LCC BV4597.57 .K56 2023 | DDC 248.4--dc23/eng/20221125
LC record available at https://lccn.loc.gov/2022045686

Cover photo by Stephan Mitchell on Unsplash

CONTENTS

PREFACE

A few years ago, a friend introduced me to a personality profile called the Enneagram. As we sat around a campfire, she began explaining her experience with it and how it was different from other personality profiles. My husband and I were familiar with various personality tests we had taken in the past, but I found the concept of the Enneagram to be extremely captivating. So I began researching the Enneagram to understand it better.

According to the Merriam-Webster online dictionary, the Enneagram is "a system of classifying personality types that is based on a nine-pointed starlike figure inscribed within a circle in which each of the nine points represents a personality type and its psychological motivations." Each of the nine personality types is assigned a number, with the Nine being the point at the top of the figure, the Eight to its left, and continuing to count down counterclockwise around the figure, until reaching the One, which is to the right of Nine. Each personality type (or number) is associated with a basic fear and a basic need. Discovering these basic fears and needs helps us better understand what motivates us to respond to the world the way we do.

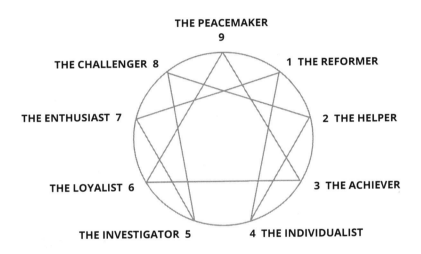

The first book I read on the Enneagram, *The Road Back to You* by Ian Cron and Suzanne Stabile, was an easy-read overview of each type and gave questions to help readers begin the process of discovering their number or personality type. This launched me on my journey toward greater awareness of the ways I had functioned on autopilot all my life. After reading the book, I took some of the free online Enneagram tests. These helped me gain insight into myself and my motivations.

The great thing about the Enneagram is that it helps reveal a pathway to growth. As I studied more about the different Enneagram types—and learned more about myself—I changed where I saw myself on the Enneagram three times. I discovered the type of person I wanted to be, the type of person I was educated (trained) to be, and the type of person I was when I wasn't thinking. As you listen to yourself and the Holy Spirit through the Enneagram, you will discover things about yourself that you never noticed. The Enneagram is not a pigeon-hole personality typing. It considers your growth, your times of waywardness, and the ways you typically think about events, people, and your experiences. To begin discovering your personality type, I suggest taking a quick online test, noting your top three numbers, and then digging into each one a little more as you go through this book.

Another great resource is to listen to some Enneagram podcasts that feature people with your top three numbers. *Typology* with Ian Morgan Cron is a great one, as well as *The Art of Growth—Enneagram Panels* by Joel Hubbard, Suzanne York, and Jim Zartman. Hearing from someone who thinks like you and can put words to how you feel is a great connection point for your Enneagram number.

Some of the textbook-type manuscripts I have studied include *The Wisdom of the Enneagram* by Don Richard Riso and Russ Hudson and *The Complete Enneagram* by Beatrice Chestnut. I've also studied many online articles. Together, these have given me a more expansive knowledge of how the Enneagram came to the United States and how it is viewed in the field of psychology. I recommend these resources only if you are interested in that aspect of the Enneagram.

As you read this book, I hope you see how your number represents an essential part of the body of Christ and recognize that God has great plans for you in building and discipling his kingdom.

INTRODUCTION

Throughout my Christian walk, I have struggled with fear. My guess is that you have struggled with fear too. In my journey toward self-awareness, I have learned that I acquired many of my fears in the guise of protection, religion, and maturity. I am just now seeing how much fear has held me back in my life and how much smaller my world became because of fear. Fear not only made my world smaller, but also made my image of God smaller. This was eye opening for me, because I want to know my God and his world in all their glory.

Studies in psychology suggest that we are born with only two fears: falling and loud noises. Some fear is rational and necessary for survival, but excessive or irrational fear keeps us from doing and being all we were created to be. In this book, I present nine common fears based on my study of the Enneagram—a personality-typing system that asserts nine basic ways people experience, interpret, and respond to their world. Each category, or personality type, has its own representative fear that binds people of that type. All of us connect in some way with most of these fears, and as you learn about them, it is likely that you will connect deeply with at least one of these fears. But God has provided us help in overcoming fear through the power of the Holy Spirit, the Comforter. In particular, the fruit of the Spirit is powerful in overcoming each fear:

But the fruit of the Spirit is love, joy, peace, patience, kindness, goodness, faithfulness, gentleness, self-control; against such things there is no law.
(Gal. 5:22–23 ESV)

My hope for you is to experience the power of the Holy Spirit as greater than the power of your fear and that this realization will guide you to an effective and productive life.

The fruit of the Spirit cannot be separated—hence, the singular *fruit*, not *fruits*. We receive all the fruit when we accept the Holy Spirit into our lives. God has provided each fruit, in part, to overcome every type of fear we face.

Here are nine common fears that people face, followed by the fruit of the Spirit that conquers those fears:

Type One: Fear of not meeting a standard—SELF-CONTROL

Type Two: Fear of being unloved—LOVE

Type Three: Fear of not doing enough—GENTLENESS

Type Four: Fear of not being good enough—GOODNESS

Type Five: Fear of not understanding or of not being understood—PATIENCE

Type Six: Fear of not being secure or safe—FAITHFULNESS

Type Seven: Fear of being alone—JOY

Type Eight: Fear of not being in control or of being controlled—KINDNESS

Type Nine: Fear of rejection—PEACE

Each chapter of this book explores one of the Enneagram types. As we look at each type, I want you to know that they are not meant to place you in a box and say, "This is how you are, so live with it." Instead, your Enneagram type is a way to observe yourself and discover what makes you who you are and how God will help you become the person he created you to be. Growth never ends. As you grow, I hope you will become stronger in your faith and use your God-given gifts to make a difference in this world. To begin growing, watch your personality in action. Occasionally, take a moment to consider, "Why did I respond in the way I did? What triggered that reaction in me? What did I do without consciously needing to think about throughout my day?"

As you read about each Enneagram type and learn more about some of the underlying motivations that cause each response, be open to learning more about your motivations.

Many of the types appear similar outwardly, but your personality type is best revealed by your motivations. It may take some time to work through why you respond the way you do. Many of us are not used to thinking deeply about our inner workings. But as we allow the Holy Spirit to lead us, he can help us learn and grow to be more Christlike.

John Wesley loved to learn about the world around him and about himself. In his words, "Experience is sufficient to confirm a doctrine which is grounded in Scripture but not sufficient to prove a doctrine which is not found in Scripture."[1] As we study the psychological aspects of our humanness, we need to weigh what we learn against Scripture. Although some criticize the Enneagram as being anti-Christian or even from Satan, I agree with religious theologian Mildred Bangs Wynkoop in *A Theology of Love*, where she asserted, "The personality is not passive, inert, but constantly meeting moments of decision which must be made in the spirit of the new life. The guarantee of grace is not that God will make these decisions for us but that we will be enabled by the Spirit to make them to please God."[2] Personality is dynamic, not static, and she describes sanctification as total moral integration of personality—the whole being uniting itself with Christ.

Sanctification is bringing about the will of God to every part of who you are. Therefore, studying who you are is an essential part of being surrendered to Christ. First Thessalonians 5:23–24 says, "May God himself, the God of peace, sanctify you through and through. May your whole spirit, soul and body be kept blameless at the coming of our Lord Jesus Christ. The one who calls you is faithful, and he will do it."

Personality is changed by the power of the Holy Spirit. A. W. Tozer wrote, "[Spirit] is different from material things, and it can penetrate personality. Your spirit can penetrate your personality. One personality can penetrate another personality. The Holy Spirit can penetrate your personality and your own spirit."[3] Relying on the power of the Holy Spirit is the key to any personality challenges we face, and knowing how to listen to him will be the source of fulfillment.

One of the first pieces of information I read on the Enneagram contained this quote by Andreas Ebert, a minister and hymn writer. He wrote, "Self-knowledge is tied with inner work, which is both demanding and painful. Change occurs amid birth pangs. It takes courage to walk such a path. Many avoid the path of self-knowledge because they are afraid of being swallowed up in their own abysses. But Christians have confidence that Christ has lived through all the abysses of human life and that he goes with us when we dare to engage in such confrontation with ourselves."[4] Observing ourselves through the lens of the Enneagram helps us know how God can work within us to become more of the person he wants us to be.

The Enneagram presents nine ways of seeing, nine ways of being, and nine ways of responding to what we see. It is broken down into three triads, each having three types of reactions, which then have three subtypes of expression. The three triads are the Body center, Head center, and Heart center. The Body center includes the Eights, Nines, and Ones. The Head center is the Fives, Sixes, and Sevens. The Heart center is the Twos, Threes, and Fours.

Briefly, people who fit into the Head center view the world through their *minds*. They do a lot of thinking, although it is not always productive thinking. They experience the world through their minds. People who register in the Heart center experience the world through their *emotions*. They are not necessarily emotional people, but they tend to process life primarily through their emotions. The Body center people experience the world through the body, as an *instinctual* or *gut* feeling. Each of the types within the triad uses that center's discernment differently.

In order to facilitate looking at ourselves more deeply, I discuss spiritual disciplines that may be of help for each type. At the end of the book, you will find tools to help you with these spiritual disciplines. Feel free to copy those pages or format them however it works for you. They are just ideas. If you already have something that works for you to connect and grow in the power of the Holy Spirit, please continue using it.

TYPE ONE

THE REFORMER

Fear: I cannot meet a standard; I am not good.
Verse to Memorize: But God demonstrates his own love for us in this: While we were still sinners, Christ died for us. (Rom. 5:8)

TYPE ONE OVERVIEW

Type One is known as the Reformer. This type is in the Body triad, meaning that people with this Enneagram number have an instinct-based personality. A One is typically self-controlled, professional, perfectionistic, purposeful, and has high moral principles. They can be crusaders for good causes. They strive to do the right thing, based on what *they* believe is right. They tend to see circumstances from a black-and-white perspective and fear making mistakes. They are also afraid of failing to measure up or perform tasks in the best way they think they can.

A unique characteristic of type One is having what is known as an inner critic. Most of us have conversations with ourselves and sometimes rethink what we have said or done. We may look back at something we did and see ways we could have done better. But Ones hear their inner voice critiquing things they have said, done, or thought about 90 percent of the time. They focus not only on self-critique but critiquing those around them. Therefore, they can seem overly critical.

Ones can easily spot what's wrong in a situation and try to make it right. Their motivation is wanting to make things better, whether a person, the world around them, or a situation they see as needing to be fixed. A problem, however, is that their inner voice establishes an ideal that is unlikely to ever be met. Ones tend to struggle with self-image, because they can't ever make themselves be how they think they should be. Even when they do something well, they find ways to criticize it. They have a hard time seeing their talents because they feel like they're always falling short.

The One's time orientation is the present. Even though their inner critic is looking at what they have done (past), they tend to focus on what's happening in the present. They strive to improve—whether that's improving themselves, helping others improve, or improving a situation. At their best, they can be discerning and wise, observing the world in unique ways. At their worst, they can be resentful, frustrated, and angry. In fact, anger is the passion (the emotional pattern or reaction) of the type One, perceived more as frustration. In a One's mind, anger is a negative or bad emotion; therefore, they try to stifle it, often becoming frustrated and resentful. As that strong emotion builds inside, sometimes bursts of anger come out.

The One's preferred center is *doing*. Because they are part of the Body triad, doing is important to them. They are productive and usually very active.

THE THREE SUBTYPES OF ONES

Like all Enneagram types, type Ones tend toward one of three subtypes: the self-preservation One, the social One, or the sexual (also known as the Intimate or One-To-One subtype) One. Each Enneagram type is influenced by the instinctual force that drives how a person is naturally drawn to survive in this world. The self-preservation instinct strives to feel safe, secure, and comfortable. This subtype will try to manage their life to avoid becoming anxious or overwhelmed. The social instinctual force strives to belong and wants to bring value to their relationships. They are socially aware of the group they are in and whom to befriend within their surroundings. The sexual instinctual force seeks to have greater intimacy and excitement in relationships. They seek to build strong bonds with individuals, whether that be friends or sexual partners. The way these instinctual forces interact with each Enneagram type affects how it is worked out in each person's survival demands.

The Self-Preservation One

Self-preservation Ones are focused primarily on themselves. They are perfectionists and want to be better. They easily see where they are lacking and try to overcome their faults.

The Social One

The social One is focused primarily on causes or fighting injustice. They want to make the world a better place, so they find ways to do that. They can be advocates for people and join causes that, from their viewpoint, will help make the world a better place.

The Sexual One

The sexual One wants to reform another person. It could be a friend, their spouse, or someone they just met. They feel like this person should want to be better, so they believe they are justified in putting pressure on them to be a better person. They can be very critical without thinking they are. In their minds, they are just trying to help. They tend to be more outgoing and energetic than the other Ones.

WHAT ONES FEAR MOST

Have you ever felt like you have fallen short of an ideal—like you cannot live up to a standard you or others expect of you? The standard—real or imagined—is so unattainable that it can never be reached; therefore, no one measures up. Type Ones can be overly critical of themselves as well as those around them. The greatest fear of the One is failing to measure up.

The law was like this for the Jews. The Pharisees had set rule after rule, until it was impossible to live up to the law. But then there was Jesus! Jesus came to fulfill the law. He came to take away the burden of trying to be perfect in the eyes of the religious leaders. We have religious leaders, even in our time, who set a standard over us that is impossible to measure up to. The fear of falling short strips us of the joy that Jesus brought.

He gave us the Holy Spirit, who gives us his power, love, and cleansing. The fruit of the Spirit includes the joy of life, the peace of knowing his love for us will never fade, and the patience we need as we journey on the road marked out for us.

Freedom in Christ does not mean that we have no law to uphold; rather, it means that the One who already upheld it is living each day with us. So, to say that one does not measure up is a lie; the Holy Spirit wants to replace it with the truth of God's love for us. We don't have to meet a standard to be part of God's family. We only need to trust in Jesus and follow the leading of the Holy Spirit in our lives. To overcome their greatest fear, Ones need to focus their minds on their connection with the Spirit.

ONES IN THE BIBLE

Was Moses an Enneagram One? I don't know, but I do believe Moses struggled with the fear of measuring up. First, he was a Hebrew raised in the Egyptian pharaoh's home, where the standard to achieve was high. He made mistakes, knew he wasn't helping his people, and ran away because he couldn't meet either standard—those of the pharaoh's household or the Hebrews. In his Egyptian home, Pharaoh set the standard, but Moses was not Egyptian by birth. From the palace, he watched his people, the Hebrew slaves, suffer and he knew that they needed help. But when faced with his first opportunity to help, he ended up murdering an Egyptian slave overseer and then running away.

In the wilderness, for the next forty years, he married, worked, and made a name for himself. Then God called him to deliver his people from their slavery in Egypt. Moses gave five excuses, trying to worm his way out of God's calling. First, he asked, "Who am I?" He didn't believe he was the person to do the job. Second, he asked God, "Who should I say sent me, if the Hebrews ask?" God answered. Question three: "What if they do not believe me or listen to me?" and again God answered him. After hearing the power of God and what God's plan was, Moses came up with excuse number four. "I have never been eloquent, neither in the past nor since you have spoken to your servant. I am slow of speech and tongue." The Lord reassured him again that he was the one for the task. Moses gave one more request: "Please, send someone else." Moses didn't believe he could meet the standard of speaking and leading the people out of slavery. So, God gave him a speaker, Aaron. As the story continued, Moses did most of the talking, but he still didn't think he could fulfill what God was asking of him. Still, God empowered Moses and gave him the words to speak to Pharaoh. Moses led his people out of Egypt. The story didn't end there. He continued to lead the Hebrews for forty more years, through many trials and marvelous events you can read about in the Bible books of Exodus, Leviticus, Deuteronomy, and Numbers.

GROWTH FOR ONES

But the fruit of the Spirit is love, joy, peace, patience,
kindness, goodness, faithfulness, gentleness,
self-control; against such things there is no law.
(Gal. 5:22–23 ESV)

The fruit of the Spirit is where growth starts for every Enneagram number. Enneagram Ones outwardly exhibit self-control in most areas of their lives. However, self-control seems not to apply to their thoughts. The only way they can take their thought lives captive is through the power of the Holy Spirit: "The mind governed by the flesh is death, but the mind governed by the Spirit is life and peace" (Rom. 8:6).

It's said that the battle is in the mind, so we must take control of that inner voice that accuses us. Granted, it's much easier said than done. Second Corinthians 10:5 tells us how: "We demolish arguments and every pretension that sets itself up against the knowledge of God, and we take captive every thought to make it obedient to Christ."

This can be a hard process, especially when that voice is constantly critiquing everything you do. It becomes wearing on your joy and peace. Discerning that critiquing voice from the Holy Spirit's voice is key. Some people set up a counter-argument for when the inner voice makes accusations, so they can respond with the truth of God's love for them. Others take a more light-hearted approach, laughing at that voice and saying, "Really? You think that could actually happen?" Not taking that voice so personally may sound weird, since it's inside your head—a part of you that has been there your whole life. You have become strangely comfortable listening to that voice, but for Ones, controlling that voice is key.

The first step is to recognize it. When do you notice that critical voice more? When does it stop you from doing something? How does it affect your relationships? How does it affect your self-image? Once you recognize its condemnation, you can correctly respond to it.

Remember, nobody's perfect. Your friends are not perfect, neither are your family members or coworkers. You are not perfect, and that's okay. Accept the fact that you're going to make mistakes. You are not going to always get it right. Be okay with that. Replace the accusing voice with this affirmation: "I did my best, and it's okay." Accepting this truth is a major growth point for Ones.

Are you often correcting those around you? Once you take note of how much you correct others, you may begin to realize why people sometimes respond to you negatively.

Now is a good time to note that, since God made us complex beings, we can see a little bit of ourselves in every Enneagram number. The Enneagram helps us not just by knowing what number we are but helps us identify those attitudes, traits, and fears that are holding us back from being all that God wants us to be. In this way, the Enneagram has been a great tool for many.

If you don't know what number you are yet, that's okay. Focus on watching how you react when responding to people or circumstances. What are your instincts? For example, Ones try to control anger because they think anger is a bad emotion. "I'm not going to let anger come out; I'm going to stuff it down deep." This will not help, because anger will eventually be expressed in a burst of unproductive emotion. Instead, think through the process: "How can I effectively deal with all of the emotions that God has given me?" Instead of denying the anger, say, "Okay, I'm angry. Why am I angry? Do I need to talk to somebody about what's triggering my anger? Is it an expectation I shouldn't have?" Take time to listen to who you are and why you do what you do. Thinking through those questions will help you grow.

The Holy Spirit wants us to grow into more than what we are, and he's given us so many tools. Scripture, prayer, meditation, silence, and the other spiritual disciplines are designed to help us.

The Enneagram One is a powerful person who can change the world for Christ. We need Ones in the world. Living under the guidance of the Holy Spirit—when they are healthy and strong—Ones can be bold and courageous. They are willing to take a stand and to sacrifice for what is right and good. When they are driven by grace, instead of guilt, they are world changers.

To help you in these growth steps, here are some spiritual disciplines Ones may want to focus on.

THE SPIRITUAL DISCIPLINES
FOR ONES

The spiritual practices that may be easiest for Ones are meditation and service. Because they feel there is a high standard to live by, meditating on God's Word helps them appreciate the standards that God has for them and his desire to make their world of influence a better place. They can live free from the power and penalty of sin. Meditating can come easy to Ones.

Service is another practice that may come more easily to Ones, because they are the reformers who like to make the world a better place. But the key is to make sure they are motivated by the love God has for them rather than performing to try to earn God's love. This is a huge mindset difference for the Ones: serving *because* God loves them rather than serving *so that* God will love them. God's love for us is not dependent on our performance. "Because he first loved us" (1 John 4:19) is the switch that the Ones must understand (actually, we all do!). This means that he loves us when we were not and are not perfect.

Confession, silence, and solitude are disciplines or practices that may challenge the Ones. Confession solidifies what they already know about themselves—that they are not perfect—by speaking that truth to God. Confession can feel degrading to Ones. It requires inner confrontation, which they may not know how to deal with. The learning comes when the Ones understand that even in their imperfections, God loves them and doesn't want them to go on their growth journey alone. Allowing other people into our lives and confessing to them and God the struggles we face will clarify the fact that we are loved even in the struggle.

Silence and solitude can also be particularly helpful. For Ones, to be silent is extremely hard because of the effort required to shut down the inner critic, to slow down and reorient themselves to listening to the Holy Spirit's voice, and to discern which voice is which. We are to put to death condemnation that comes from within. Taking captive every thought is constant work for Ones. Getting that inner critic crucified with Christ and allowing the Holy Spirit to speak instead is where the work comes in. Take time to learn how God speaks to you and know that Christ did not come to condemn the world but to save it. That applies to you. Condemnation never comes from the Holy Spirit. God sees you and loves you, even when you feel unworthy and faulty. That is what the Ones need to hold on to. When you are meditating, serving, confessing, and practicing silence and solitude, remember that God sees you, knows all about you, and loves you enough to die for you.

The world needs you. As a One, don't ever give up because when you find your purpose, nothing will be able to stop you. You can change your world because of the gifts God has given you. Stay committed.

QUESTIONS FOR A ONE

1. Do I know my inner critic? Can I recognize the inner, condemning voice?

2. Do I know the voice of the Holy Spirit? Can I hear the comforting, loving voice of God as I go through my day?

3. When do I feel frustrated? Is it because I have failed at something? Is it because I am angry at someone?

4. When do I feel resentful? Is it because someone else didn't do something well? Is it because I am always the one to correct things done wrong?

5. What brings me joy?

6. What brings me peace?

7. When do I feel most in control?

8. When do I allow God to be in control?

QUESTIONS FOR THOSE WHO WORK
OR LIVE WITH A ONE

1. How can I give grace to someone who always feels like they never get it right?

2. How do I show that I value the integrity of doing my best in everything I do?

3. The One desires organization. How can I keep the area the One and I share organized and clean? Am I showing that I am willing to value the things they value?

4. Support a cause the One in your life values and voice appreciation for his or her devotion to making the world a better place.

5. Ones need encouragement in the form of *specific* compliments that they are doing a good job to counteract the critical voice they hear all the time. How can I encourage them? What specific things can I compliment them on?

6. In what ways can I remind them that God's love for them is not based on what they do?

VERSES FOR MEDITATION FOR ONES

The Story of Naaman
2 Kings 5:1–19

. . . . .

He says, "Be still, and know that I am God; I will be
exalted among the nations, I will be exalted in the earth."
Psalm 46:10

. . . . .

You, Lord, are forgiving and good,
abounding in love to all who call to you.
Psalm 86:5

. . . . .

He has caused his wonders to be remembered;
the Lord is gracious and compassionate.
Psalm 111:4

. . . . .

To all perfection I see a limit,
but your commands are boundless.
Psalm 119:96

. . . . .

My heart is not proud, LORD, my eyes are not haughty;
I do not concern myself with great matters or
things too wonderful for me. But I have calmed and
quieted myself, I am like a weaned child with its mother;
like a weaned child I am content. Israel, put your hope
in the LORD both now and forevermore.

Psalm 131

. . . . .

The Parable of the Weeds
Matthew 13:24–30

. . . . .

His intent was that now, through the church, the
manifold wisdom of God should be made known to the
rulers and authorities in the heavenly realms, according
to his eternal purpose that he accomplished in Christ
Jesus our Lord. In him and through faith in him we may
approach God with freedom and confidence.

Ephesians 3:10–12

. . . . .

But he said to me, "My grace is sufficient for you,
for my power is made perfect in weakness." Therefore
I will boast all the more gladly about my weaknesses,
so that Christ's power may rest on me.

2 Corinthians 12:9

. . . . .

TYPE TWO

THE HELPER

Fear: Being unwanted or unworthy of being loved

Verse to Memorize: The LORD your God is with you, the Mighty Warrior who saves. He will take great delight in you; in his love he will no longer rebuke you, but will rejoice over you with singing. (Zeph. 3:17)

TYPE TWO OVERVIEW

The Enneagram Two is known as the Helper. Women who take the short online Enneagram tests often find that Two is one of their numbers. This seems to be especially true of Christian women. This is likely because many of the Two's attributes have been taught in the church as to how Christian women are to be. Many of us have been trained in the helper mindset; therefore, in answering the questions on a quiz, we'll often score as a Two, not because it's our natural ability but because of the training that has become part of our thinking. So, as we look at the Two, be sure to evaluate if this is your natural response or learned behavior.

Type Two is in the Heart (feeling) triad, and the orientation to time is the present. People designated as Twos focus on what is happening right now. Their passion is pride, an unexpected trait for a person who is helpful and generous. But pride is their downfall, because they please others as the way to evoke affection from them. To win others' approval through indirect methods—such as seduction, manipulation, and strategic giving—is their way to obtain emotional and material support without having to ask for it. They want people to help them, without having to ask for help, because they fear being told no, being rejected.

Twos often adopt an elevated or an idealized view of themselves and think they can help everybody. They often have a hard time saying no, when asked to help, because they feel like they're the ones who can do it. They appear generous, helpful, attractive, and supportive. They are great friends, but they subconsciously create that inviting front so that others will need them. If Twos create in others a need for them, Twos assume that others will, in turn, meet their needs. Twos have an underlying feeling that, since they notice your needs and help you, you should notice their needs and help them as well. Because they are good at seeing people's needs, they expect others to reciprocate. Other Enneagram types tend to be not as good at spotting others' needs, so

Twos' needs often go unmet, causing them to struggle. They often don't ask for help, because they believe that the people around them should just intuitively know what they need.

Empathizing with people is a strength for the type Two, and they have an amazing ability to listen to people. They are cheerful, optimistic, and diplomatic. They sugarcoat the truth and make it sound good. They don't like to hurt people's feelings, so they choose to look at the optimistic side of an event and find the good in people. Reciprocity is their survival strategy. Even if they do not realize what they are doing, they give to get.

THE THREE SUBTYPES OF TWOS

Like Ones, Twos fall under one of three subtypes.

The Self-Preservation Two

The self-preservation Two is the counter type. It reflects a childlike personality that presents oneself as innocent, adorable, and cute, so that others will want to help them and meet their needs. They tend to give themselves to others to remain the favorite, the cutest, or the one who is the neediest. But they also want to be unique, as well as liked by everyone around them. They're more guarded and less trusting than the other Two subtypes. Sometimes, they are perceived as having an invisible wall as protection for when others are trying to go deeper in connection with them. They have a sense of self-importance, just as a child who thinks she is the most important person in the room. As adults, they can appear irresponsible, playful, and as charming as a child. They don't want to have to take care of themselves, so they put on that childlike charm, so that others will take care of them.

This subtype of Two can resemble an Enneagram type Six, since they are fearful of individual relationships. They can also resemble a type Four in that they are emotional and want to be loved, but they try to meet others' needs for that love. The self-preservation Two will focus more on others in trying to manipulate the situation to get their needs met.

The Social Two

The social Two is the more adult type. They are leaders, take pride in influencing others, and feel they are better than everybody else. They are ambitious and tend to know the right people. They accomplish meaningful change in their communities and are usually admired for their accomplishments. Their pride consists in how much of an audience they capture. They subconsciously believe that everybody wants to be like them and that they are the standard. They use strategic giving and generosity, especially when they're in groups, to get people on their side and gain respect. They apply this strategic angle whenever they are generous, but their "generosity" is giving to get.

Social Twos are private and introverted, more so than the other two subtypes. Because they portray being the leader and want everybody to admire them, they don't want people to know their real selves. They don't want others to see them with their guard down, so they tend to pull back from close relationships. They protect their public image.

People of this subtype deny their vulnerable emotions—shame, fear, mistrust, jealousy, and envy—referring to them as negative. Therefore, they deny them, refusing to acknowledge that they have them.

This subtype of Two can resemble a Three or an Eight, because they are goal-oriented, very much in charge, but tend to be a little bit warmer and more caring than the Three, and they are much more easily accessible to their emotions than the Eight. They tend to be more generous, giving, and supportive of others, even though the motive is subconsciously to get something.

The Sexual Two

The sexual Two is the seducer in the physical sense. They are usually very friendly, upbeat, and focused on relationships. They desire strong connections with individuals and target specific individuals with their generosity and flexibility. They are somewhat wild and not afraid to woo people, using sexuality as a weapon of conquest. They want to look beautiful, and they want others to think that they are beautiful. They can be direct, dramatic, and aggressive. It is one-on-one connection they seek, wanting somebody to desire them so much that they'll do anything for them. Seduction is how sexual Twos get their needs met. They target their seduction to get one person to be willing to do whatever they need them to do, will not take no for an answer, don't set boundaries well, and don't like to be rejected. Rejection would be the ultimate pain for this Two.

Because of their "wild at heart" actions, they may be mistyped as a Four.

WHAT TWOS FEAR MOST

The basic fear of the type Two is being unwanted and unworthy of being loved. They might feel undeserving of love and relationships. Therefore, their basic desire is to be loved. This fear drives them to do whatever is necessary to win the love and acceptance of others. They find it hard to express their need to others, so they try to make others feel indebted to them to create an expectation of acceptance. However, when the Spirit steps in and begins to work with the Two, they find that the love they have been seeking is in Christ. When they grab hold of that love and experience Christ's acceptance, they can use their gifts and abilities to share that acceptance with others.

TWOS IN THE BIBLE

Was Martha a Two? Again, we have no way of knowing the inner heart of Martha, but she exhibited some of the outward characteristics of the Two, as indicated in Luke 10:38–42:

As Jesus and his disciples were on their way, he came to a village where a woman named Martha opened her home to him. She had a sister called Mary, who sat at the Lord's feet listening to what he said. But Martha was distracted by all the preparations that had to be made. She came to him and asked, "Lord, don't you care that my sister has left me to do the work by myself? Tell her to help me!" "Martha, Martha," the Lord answered, "you are worried and upset about many things, but few things are needed—or indeed only one. Mary has chosen what is better, and it will not be taken away from her."

Who opened their home to Jesus? Who was working hard to make sure all the preparations were done? Who did not ask her sister for help but let resentment and bitterness build until she became angry and asked Jesus to intervene? Martha. We love her heart for service and her willingness to open her home, but she was missing out on the important thing that was happening. Martha wanted her work to be noticed and did not want to ask for help when she felt she was doing it all on her own. We all need helpers (Twos) in our lives, and they have much to offer the church, but Jesus also wanted Martha to enjoy the time with him.

Serving is a gift and is one of the things that makes Christians stand out among the takers. But if serving is done with strings attached, it loses its effectiveness.

GROWTH FOR TWOS

But the fruit of the Spirit is love, joy, peace, patience,
kindness, goodness, faithfulness, gentleness,
self-control; against such things there is no law.
(Gal. 5:22–23 ESV)

The fruit of the Spirit is where growth starts for every number. Twos naturally exhibit love; however, it seems that that they never receive love themselves. Twos would do well to understand that the love the Holy Spirit gives is the only love that allows us to love others with no strings attached. This is where the Two will see growth. Allowing the Holy Spirit to show them how much they are loved by God and then being able to love those around them unconditionally will fulfill them in a new and fresh way. In his letter to the Ephesians, Paul wrote his prayer for the people:

I pray that out of his glorious riches he may strengthen you with power through his Spirit in your inner being, so that Christ may dwell in your hearts through faith. And I pray that you, being rooted and established in love, may have power, together with all the Lord's holy people, to grasp how wide and long and high and deep is the love of Christ, and to know this love that surpasses knowledge—that you may be filled to the measure of all the fullness of God. (Eph. 3:16–19)

If you're a Two, observe when you automatically say yes to someone's request. Ask yourself, "Can I really do this? Is this something I'm able to help with? Do I have time to help with this, and can I follow through on it?" Twos are others-oriented, so thinking through what they themselves are feeling and what they give their attention to is a big step in growth.

For Twos, knowing how to voice that you need help or that you need something from somebody is another area of growth. Have you evaluated if you need help completing a project or keeping up with everything happening in your family? It can be exhausting trying to keep up the appearance of having it all together when you are driving three kids to sporting events, running the household, doing the laundry and cooking, let alone helping others. Learn to be more direct in what you need or want.

My husband and I talk about this in our marriage counseling with couples. Too often, Twos mistakenly assume that people know what they need and want. As an example, a Two may help somebody move into a new house, but when Twos need to move, they assume people will be there to help without having to be asked to help. In couples, the wife may think that the husband should know that she needs a hug, to be cuddled, or to watch a movie. But the husband is clueless. He doesn't know how to see the need. He needs to be told or asked to meet that need.

Remember, not everyone is as intuitive as you are, so you may need to be more direct in voicing your needs. As people learn how generous you are with your time and abilities, they tend to ask more of you. A beginning growth step might be to say "maybe" rather than "yes," when asked to help. Think about the time and commitment helping would take. Ask the questions above to help determine if you can or even want to take on that responsibility and how it might take your attention and energy from something else.

The last thing is to become more aware of how you use strategic generosity. Why are you helping? Is it from a heart of generosity, or is there some underlying expectation? Thinking this through is a huge growing step for Twos.

We are called to be generous, and the Twos who have taken the time to grow are some of the greatest leaders in generosity. Twos are naturally able to recognize needs and have a great capacity to fulfill them. But the Spirit of God looks at their motivation and heart. When Twos are spiritually healthy, they draw people to them, making people feel recognized and understood. They draw out the good in others and help people see their worth. To help you in these growth steps, the following are some spiritual disciplines you may want to focus on.

THE SPIRITUAL DISCIPLINES
FOR TWOS

Prayer and service are practices that may come easy for Twos. I include prayer because they can see other people's needs so easily, and they are great at bringing those requests and petitions before the Lord. What doesn't come easy in prayer for the Two is bringing their own needs and desires before Christ. Twos need to be willing to acknowledge their needs before Christ and verbalize their struggles through prayer. So, prayer can be both easy and challenging for Twos.

Service comes easy to Twos because they love being helpers. They want to help people. They see their needs and can be very generous, sometimes even overdoing the help when people don't necessarily want or need it. They can be a servant, but they need to work on the motivation for their serving. Is it out of love for God and a desire to make God known? Or is it because they want their own needs met and need to be needed? Twos must be aware of their motivation.

Meditation, fasting, and study may be the challenging practices for the type Two. Meditating on God's Word is taking a word, verse, fragment, or phrase and thinking about it, its meaning, and its application, and then internalizing it. Meditation is challenging for Twos, because they are always looking at what other people need, while failing to notice what God wants to teach them. So, they must go beyond thinking about how this section of God's Word is helpful for this or that person and instead consider how it is helpful for themselves.

Fasting may be difficult for Twos because it highlights their basic needs. When one of those basic needs is taken away—for example, food—they have to rely on God. They must rely on his strength and comfort, while letting him be all that they need.

Study may be a challenge, because Twos are in the Heart triad. They don't like the thinking aspect of being God's child.

They prefer the feelings and emotions that are attached to faith. To study, mentally process, and learn deeper truths is hard work. This is not because they're not smart, but because study it is not their instinct, or enjoyable. The mental energy required to go deeper in God's Word can feel beyond their ability.

The key thought to remember for the type Two is that God can use the service others do for you to bless you. Allow others to serve you. Give up your shame for expressing your needs. Just as you enjoy helping others, others enjoy helping too. Helpers are blessed when serving, so to refuse their help can deny them this blessing. To illustrate, when Jesus wanted to wash Peter's feet, Peter was not having any of that. He felt unworthy to have Jesus wash his feet. But Jesus said, "Unless I wash you, you have no part with me" (John 13:8). God wants us to accept what he wants to do for us and in us, as well as what he wants us to do for him. Accept that he has others serving for him, and that might include doing something for you.

The world needs you. You have the part of God's character that serves. You will be the one who helps whenever possible. The church can learn so much from your servant's heart. What we need from you is to let us help you. You love to serve, but we want you to also be willing to be served.

QUESTIONS FOR A TWO

1. When am I able to say that I love myself unconditionally? Do I believe that I am lovable? Why or why not?

2. How do I establish healthy boundaries between myself and others?

3. When am I willing to acknowledge my "negative" emotions (shame, fear, mistrust, jealousy, and envy)?

4. How am I clear about my intentions when helping or giving?

5. How do I express what I need?

6. What brings me joy?

7. Do I seek God in using my time and resources? Why or why not?

QUESTIONS FOR THOSE WHO WORK OR LIVE WITH A TWO

1. How do I express my appreciation for Twos in my life?

2. When am I taking the time to get to know them personally?

3. How can I notice if they are overworked or feeling stressed out?

4. When do I ask them what they need or desire?

VERSES FOR MEDITATION FOR TWOS

The Lord is my shepherd, I lack nothing. He makes
me lie down in green pastures, he leads
me beside quiet waters.

Psalm 23:1–2

. . . . .

You do not delight in sacrifice, or I would bring it;
you do not take pleasure in burnt offerings.
My sacrifice, O God, is a broken spirit; a broken
and contrite heart you, God, will not despise.

Psalm 51:16–17

. . . . .

Woe to those who go down to Egypt for help, who rely on
horses, who trust in the multitude of their chariots and in
the great strength of their horsemen, but do not look to
the Holy One of Israel, or seek help from the Lord.

Isaiah 31:1

. . . . .

So do not fear, for I am with you; do not be dismayed, for
I am your God. I will strengthen you and help you; I will
uphold you with my righteous right hand.

Isaiah 41:10

. . . . .

Come, all you who are thirsty, come to the waters; and you
who have no money, come, buy and eat! Come, buy wine
and milk without money and without cost.

Isaiah 55:1

．　．　．　．　．

The Lord your God is with you, the Mighty Warrior who
saves. He will take great delight in you; in his love he will no
longer rebuke you, but will rejoice over you with singing.

Zephaniah 3:17

．　．　．　．　．

You have heard that it was said, "Love your neighbor and
hate your enemy." But I tell you, love your enemies and
pray for those who persecute you, that you may be children of your Father in heaven. He causes his sun to rise
on the evil and the good, and sends rain on the righteous
and the unrighteous. If you love those who love you, what
reward will you get? Are not even the tax collectors doing
that? And if you greet only your own people, what are you
doing more than others? Do not even pagans do that?

Matthew 5:43–47

．　．　．　．　．

Jesus Washing the Disciples' Feet
John 13:2–11

．　．　．　．　．

I no longer call you servants, because a servant
does not know his master's business. Instead,
I have called you friends, for everything that I learned
from my Father I have made known to you.

John 15:15

. . . . .

In all these things we are more than conquerors through
him who loved us. For I am convinced that neither death
nor life, neither angels nor demons, neither the present
nor the future, nor any powers, neither height nor depth,
nor anything else in all creation, will be able to separate us
from the love of God that is in Christ Jesus our Lord.

Romans 8:37–39

. . . . .

Praise be to the God and Father of our Lord Jesus Christ,
who has blessed us in the heavenly realms with every
spiritual blessing in Christ. For he chose us in him before
the creation of the world to be holy and blameless in
his sight. In love he predestined us for adoption to
sonship through Jesus Christ, in accordance with his
pleasure and will—to the praise of his glorious grace,
which he has freely given us in the One he loves.

Ephesians 1:3–6

. . . . .

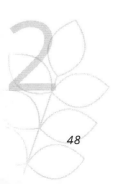

TYPE THREE

THE ACHIEVER

Fear: I don't do enough.

Verses to Memorize: God saved you by his grace when you believed. And you can't take credit for this; it is a gift from God. Salvation is not a reward for the good things we have done, so none of us can boast about it. (Eph. 2:8–9 NLT)

TYPE THREE OVERVIEW

Working through the personality type you identify with requires facing both the positives and negatives of that type. Evaluating how you subconsciously live can be an eye-opening experience—and is not always easy. Part of growing in Christ is being able to see where he wants you to grow, as well as acknowledging the gifts he has given you. Be willing to do the hard work of knowing yourself and letting the Holy Spirit work in you to make you into the Christlike person you are called to be.

Type Three is known as the Performer, Achiever, or Chameleon and is in the Heart (feeling) triad with the Twos and Fours. Three is in the middle of the triad, and each type that is in the middle of their triad represses that triad's primary characteristic. So, the Three represses feeling, the Six represses thinking, and the Nine represses the body. Therefore, Threes do not like to feel, because it could slow them down somehow. Threes believe that feelings do not get them to their desired accomplishments, so they tend to push back feelings to be able to do more. They tend to "do" to be accepted. They try to create an image of success, value, or beauty to get them the attention or applause that confirms they are loved.

Usually, they wear a social mask that changes according to the group they are with. They are very adept at scoping out a situation to figure out the social norms and standards, and then conforming to them. They are very hard workers, make good first impressions, and are likable and energetic. Because they are others-oriented, they can get caught up in who they are trying to be for others and forget who they really are. In the same way, they look to others, rather than themselves, to set standards and then they try to meet them. They are much more outward focused. How they feel about themselves is based on what others think or expect of them. If they can meet that standard, they have a higher self-image; if they can't meet it, they feel defeated and see themselves as a failure.

Obstacles irritate Threes, because they interfere with what Threes want to accomplish. They are doers and focused on accomplishing a goal for their family, group, team, or other entity. They are good at multitasking and adept at splitting their attention among several things. They are good group leaders, because they are adept at managing the various aspects of groups. Because they focus on what others think and expect, Threes do what it takes to meet those needs. However, they don't always take time to be themselves; therefore, without others' input, they are challenged to know who they are. They don't always understand that the image they portray is not who they really are, and they deceive themselves into thinking they are somebody they're not.

Threes are competitive and like to complete tasks in the fastest, shortest ways, even if that means running over people. Sometimes Threes are unaware of what they're doing to other people when pursuing their goals.

Their passion is vanity, or what some versions of the Bible call *vainglory*. This is thinking more of themselves than what they are. Because of the many images of themselves, they feel like they can fit in wherever and put themselves above others. Sometimes it is a conscious mindset while other times it is subconscious.

THE THREE SUBTYPES OF THREES

Just like other Enneagram types, there are three subtypes of Threes.

The Self-Preservation Three

The self-preservation Three is still focused and hard-working but also more likely than other subtypes to do what is right and best. They have a sense of doing their work better than anyone else, in the right way, and being a good example to others. They still like to be the center of attention, to be the leader, and to be the best—the best parent, teacher, business owner, group leader, or whatever. They not only want to project an image of being the best; they want to *be* the best, working hard to earn that.

They desire to appear attractive, virtuous, and successful without letting on that this is what they want. This is where the vainglory comes in. It's like vanity for not being vain. And so, this Three wants people to look up to them and admire them. Because they fit into the self-preservation Three, their desire is for security, which makes their lives somewhat simple.

These Threes tend to focus on the practical and useful and have no need for the outlandish or impractical. They believe, "I have to do everything, because I do it better." Ones can easily be confused with Threes, but Threes move at a much faster pace, wanting to get things done and keep things moving. Threes also are more image-conscious than Ones, who look internally for doing what's right, while Threes look externally to what others think is right. They can also be confused with Sixes, but again, are more concerned about their image, and they work harder when facing a problem. They produce to feel secure, so when encountering anything that could cause insecurities, they work hard and won't slow down—where a Six will slow down to think things through.

The Social Three

The Threes who fit into this subtype are the performers. They want to be onstage with everybody looking at them. They like the applause and attention. The mindset of "bring it on" and "give me the praise" keeps them in the spotlight. They are probably the most socially brilliant of the Threes, because they are charismatic in any situation, drawing people to them. But they are also the most competitive of the Threes—in it to win it. This subtype tends to run over people as they strive to win. They are inclined to view people as assets or obstacles, evaluating others in a situation to determine if that person is in the way or will help reach the Three's goal. Threes will develop a relationship with those who help; however, they will snub those deemed in the way. These are the most aggressive, strong, and assertive of the Threes.

The Sexual Three

The sexual Three attracts people by their beauty or appeal; people like to be around them. They are usually sweet and shy, not as extroverted as the other Threes. They tend to focus on others. Where the other Three subtypes are wanting to be the achiever, the sexual Three is the counter type, supporting others in their goals. In fact, they push others to achieve by being their cheerleader and enthusiast. Their goal is to be the best supporters, pleasers, and helpers.

They have a great fear of feeling emotional pain, so they pull back from deeper connections with people because they don't want others to know much about them. All Threes do this to a degree. They keep people at arm's length while protecting the image they have worked so hard to create.

The sexual Three can look a lot like a Two or a Seven. They are different from Twos in that they focus on being attractive rather than meeting people's needs. They are a helper because that adds to their image of being attractive and wanting people to like being around them, whereas the Two wants to be needed by other people. Sevens know what they want, but a sexual Three lets others decide what they should want. They are also not as connected with their emotions as the Seven.

WHAT THREES FEAR MOST

Threes hold the belief that their worth is wrapped up in what they do. If they are not doing, they are lazy, a burden, or selfish. In the legalistic church, which many of us were raised in, some of us were taught a list of dos and don'ts a mile long, and any straying from that meant we were walking away from God. As a Three growing up in this setting, I felt like I was never doing enough for God to accept me. There was always something I was doing (lying, cheating, drinking, lusting) or wasn't doing (reading my Bible, praying, going to church) that made me feel unworthy. The guilt and shame of that life were overwhelming. I was at the altar time after time, asking God to help me to be better. As a grown woman, it didn't get better. The Proverbs 31 woman is such an unattainable goal in my mind that I never felt like I could be worth something to God or others. My head knowledge told me that God loved me for who I was, but the pressure from my upbringing left me trying to gain God's love by doing, doing, doing.

After years of feeling that shame and guilt, I came to the transformational knowledge that God loves me and wants me to know him in a personal relationship way more than he wants me to act and think a certain way. He wants me to know his ideas about who I am and what I mean to him. Knowing him is my passion. He said time and again that knowing him was knowing the Father. If we don't have that, how do we know what to *do*?

I am not saying that I can do anything I want and still be in relationship with God. What I am saying is that, when I am in a relationship with God, the focus is not on the dos and don'ts, but on the relationship. How is he leading me to respond to him at any given moment? The dos and don'ts take care of themselves when we live that way. My life is now governed by listening to God's guidance and not the condemnation that comes from thinking, "I didn't read enough Scripture today." My relationship leads me to want to know him more, so the actions make sense as I grow closer in my relationship with him. I want to talk to him about my day, know what he thinks is important, and please him by not doing things that hinder that relationship. In other words, God's love for me is not dependent on my "doing enough for him." He loves me because he is love.

THREES IN THE BIBLE

Jacob seems to fit into a Three's pattern of behavior in many ways. Although we can never know his motivations and state of heart, he did seem to set high goals and found ways to achieve them. He devised a plan to get the birthright from Esau. He tricked his father into giving him his blessing. He set goals as a shepherd of Laban's flocks, leaving his employer a rich man. He seemed to always be working toward a goal and desiring to be successful. However, his life was full of trials and suffering. Jacob ended up doing what we all must do: he confronted his failures, his weaknesses, and his sins. After years of estrangement, he headed back to his brother Esau and encountered an angelic stranger. Jacob wrestled with God all night—an exhausting struggle that left him with a disability. It was only after he gave up the struggle and realized he could not go on without God that he received a blessing.

GROWTH FOR THREES

But the fruit of the Spirit is love, joy, peace, patience,
kindness, goodness, faithfulness, gentleness,
self-control; against such things there is no law.
(Gal. 5:22–23 ESV)

The fruit of the Spirit is where growth starts for every type. For Threes, gentleness is demonstrated in the way they encourage and spur others on to great things. However, Threes are not gentle in their comparisons of themselves with others. They see themselves as not doing enough and not being the "right" person in a given situation. To know they are loved for who they are and not for what they do is the Holy Spirit's work in their lives. They can become great leaders in spreading the good news. In his second letter to Timothy, Paul instructed, "Opponents must be gently instructed, in the hope that God will grant them repentance leading them to a knowledge of the truth" (2 Tim. 2:25).

We can ask Threes to make these observations: What seems to be the most important thing to you throughout your day? As you are in different situations, ask, "What about this is important to me?" and "Do I change how I present myself depending on who I'm with?" Noticing these specifics can bring to consciousness what has been working subconsciously in Threes for a long time. Start to notice how you are different with one person than you are with somebody else. Take note of what you do to distract yourself from certain emotions. As a Three, you tend to keep busy so you don't have to deal with your emotions.

Another growth point for the Three is to confront what failure means to you. Your self-image is based on what you're doing. Failure can lead to depression or shutting down. When facing a major failure, make sure you have compassion for yourself. No one is perfect, so giving yourself grace will be key in getting through the experience. If you have already gone through a devastating failure, find someone to talk with you to help you process those emotions.

Become more aware of when you do things strictly because they will boost your image. For example, when you don't want to do something or don't need to do it, yet you do it to make people like you more or put you in a better light, think again. Notice what types of situations or activities you do just to get that image boost. To help you in these growth steps, here are some of the spiritual disciplines you may want to focus on.

THE SPIRITUAL DISCIPLINES
FOR THREES

The spiritual disciplines that seem to come easily for Threes are prayer and study. Threes are good at setting and meeting goals. Having a set time to do prayer and Bible study is a great plan for their growth. They set out to accomplish these times and can enjoy growth if they focus on learning and not just going through the motions to check the task off the list. They like to study and learn new things, but sometimes they fail to work through the emotional part of the growth process. So, for Threes, prayer and study times can reveal more, if they are willing to engage their emotions.

What can also make times of prayer and study a bit more challenging is that Threes tend to do them to be seen by others. So maybe they have a Bible or prayer app that includes friends who can see when they do a Bible study or view their prayer list. Threes can become proud of their success and that people know what they are doing. In some ways, the app holds them accountable, but it can also build their self-image. They can get caught up in prayer and study for the wrong reason. So, again, even the practices a person is good at will have its challenges, when considering their motivation.

Three practices that can be more challenging for Threes: confession, fasting, and simplicity. Confession is hard for Threes, because they don't like people to know that they aren't measuring up, aren't in control, or are faulty in some way. They feel that confession will hurt their image, when, in fact, as a Christian, confession helps us grow and become more confident in our faith. We all have faults, so confession can help how people relate to Threes. Knowing that they have struggles and are not always confident and successful can help others grow as well. Admitting they struggle can profoundly grow Threes' ability to rely on God.

Fasting can be difficult for Threes, because they get can caught up in doing it to be seen by others rather being seen only by God. Fasting is often thought of as withholding food, but for Threes, fasting from social media could be more beneficial. Taking time away from social media to look inward and focus on their spiritual lives would be a great way for them to use fasting to grow closer to God.

Living simply, or simplicity, is very hard for the Threes because they like the appearance of success. In our society, success is evident in possessions and looking the part. Having things brings people status in our culture. Letting go of material things that take Threes' time and attention away from their spiritual lives can help them grow in their faith.

Other practices that can help the Threes grow don't require *doing* anything. Meditation and the practice of silence are huge growth opportunities for Threes, though they are difficult. If you're a Three, take time to let God speak to you, and when emotions emerge, don't shut them down. Sit still and listen to God, listen to his Word, without doing anything. Find a place that works for you to sit and listen to what the Holy Spirit speaks.

A great verse for the type Three is 1 Corinthians 13:1: "If I speak in tongues of men or of angels, but do not have love, I am only a resounding gong or a clanging cymbal." The key thought for Threes to remember is, *I don't need to present a successful, accomplished person to Christ; he focuses on the heart and why I am doing what I am doing. He loves me even when he sees every part of my heart.* This statement understands that we can't put on a front and deceive God. He sees who we are—including our motives and our hearts—and he loves us anyway. Grasping the fact that God loves us for who we are, not for what we do, is a truth a Three can hold on to.

The world needs you. Your gift is truthfulness and authenticity. You can see through the games people play. You value honesty and are good at seeing the world as it could be. You can see how to make things better. You are efficient and find ways of getting things done in a faster, more effective way.

QUESTIONS FOR A THREE

1. How do I let my accomplishments define me?

2. Who am I most authentic with? Why?

3. When do I take time to work through the tougher emotions?

4. When do I allow God to be in control?

5. What brings me joy?

6. How am I willing to give myself grace when I fail? How do I give others grace when they fail?

7. What have I deceived myself into believing about myself? Why?

QUESTIONS FOR THOSE WHO WORK OR LIVE WITH A THREE

1. How am I clear and direct with my needs and wants?

2. How can I be focused and concise when sharing with them?

3. How do I convey that I value them for who they are and not what they do for me?

4. How can I help them accomplish a goal or give praise when they've reached a goal?

5. In what ways can I remind them that God's love does not depend on how much they do?

VERSES FOR MEDITATION FOR THREES

But the Lord said to Samuel, "Do not consider his
appearance or his height, for I have rejected him.
The Lord does not look at the things people
look at. People look at the outward appearance,
but the Lord looks at the heart."

1 Samuel 16:7

. . . . .

All Creation Is Called to Praise the Lord

Psalm 148

. . . . .

Be careful not to practice your righteousness in front
of others to be seen by them. If you do, you will have no
reward from your Father in heaven. So when you give
to the needy, do not announce it with trumpets, as the
hypocrites do in the synagogues and on the streets, to be
honored by others. Truly I tell you, they have received their
reward in full. But when you give to the needy, do not
let your left hand know what your right hand is doing,
so that your giving may be in secret. Then your Father,
who sees what is done in secret, will reward you.

Matthew 6:1–4

. . . . .

Come to me, all you who are weary and burdened,
and I will give you rest. Take my yoke upon you
and learn from me, for I am gentle and humble
in heart, and you will find rest for your souls.
For my yoke is easy and my burden is light.

Matthew 11:28–30

. . . . .

This is what the kingdom of God is like. A man
scatters seed on the ground. Night and day, whether he
sleeps or gets up, the seed sprouts and grows, though
he does not know how. All by itself the soil produces
grain—first the stalk, then the head, then the full
kernel in the head. As soon as the grain is ripe, he puts
the sickle to it, because the harvest has come.

Mark 4:26–29

. . . . .

As a prisoner for the Lord, then, I urge you to live a life
worthy of the calling you have received. Be completely
humble and gentle; be patient, bearing with one another in
love. Make every effort to keep the unity of the Spirit
through the bond of peace. There is one body and one
Spirit, just as you were called to one hope when you were
called; one Lord, one faith, one baptism; one God and
Father of all, who is over all and through all and in all.

Ephesians 4:1–6

. . . . .

Whatever you do, work at it with all your heart,
as working for the Lord, not for human masters.
Colossians 3:23

. . . . .

3

TYPE FOUR

THE INDIVIDUALIST

Fear: Rejection

Verses to Memorize: We are hard pressed on every side, but not crushed; perplexed, but not in despair; persecuted, but not abandoned; struck down, but not destroyed. . . . Therefore we do not lose heart. (2 Cor. 4:8–9, 16)

TYPE FOUR OVERVIEW

Type Four, known as the Individualist, is part of the Heart (feeling) triad with types Two and Three. Fours are probably the most emotional of the Heart triad. They feel emotions deeply, are sensitive and introspective, and can be expressive and dramatic. They express their emotions easily, even experiencing a range of emotions in a short time, which can overwhelm them. They are creative and emotionally honest with God. They are compassionate, sensing other people's emotional state. They're great listeners and emotionally strong for others, making them good support for those who are going through difficult circumstances.

Their passion is envy, which comes out in three distinct ways, which we'll cover in the subtypes section. They become envious of others who have something they desire, even if they cannot precisely identify what that "thing" is. They feel like they're missing out on something.

Fours are the artistic, romantic type. What stands out among Fours is their connection to emotions, particularly grief and sadness. If they let themselves focus on the sadness and hurt around them, they can fall into depression and hopelessness. They tend to give themselves over to melancholy feelings more often than joyful feelings.

Fours see themselves as unique and special. These qualities make them want to stand out in the crowd, even though most are introverted. They have a great need to be seen by others, because they desire to be loved, yet they don't feel they deserve to be loved, believing they're not worth it. It becomes counterproductive, because they seek love, but when people try to love them, they tend to become stand-offish.

Fours can be self-absorbed and temperamental, even to the point of being okay with sadness. They tend to be introverted and are often intellectual, using their intellect to work through their emotions. They have a natural ability to see a situation at a deeper emotional level than most other types and can perceive underlying emotions of people, a situation, or a relationship. They can be beautiful, wonderful, talented people, having a great ability to see the beauty in everything, seeing the world in unique and special ways. But they typically have a low view of themselves, because they feel like they are lacking. They believe that something is missing in their lives, but they can never identify it.

Their defense mechanism is introjection. If someone a Four respects criticizes him or her, the Four introjects that person within themselves, so that the outside criticism becomes an internal criticism, part of the Four's inner voice. If they internalize it, they can control it, even though it replays in their minds. It then creates an inner critic, similar to the type One's experience.

THE THREE SUBTYPES OF FOURS

As we discuss the three subtypes of the Four, we will look at the way their envy comes out in suffering.

The Self-Preservation Four

This subtype is the counter type for the Four. The self-preservation Four's reaction to envy is to become long-suffering. They envy what others have, but suffer silently, believing they will never be complete. They don't want people to know that they are suffering, so they suffer in silence, suppressing and internalizing what they need. They learn to endure pain without complaining or whining;

they "suck it up and move on." They appear stoic and strong, but they suffer, while feeling shame and envy that they rarely communicate to others.

These Fours strive to live a life of drama to be extraordinary. They take high risks that may put them in danger for the sake of being special. Feeling like a victim, they may feel that no one has it as bad as they do. They become depressed or believe they are invincible. They think that if they die, it will make everyone realize how special they were. However, when a crisis does hit, they are typically the one who works like no other to help make the situation right.

Self-preservation Fours see themselves as the hero in a story. When they are in a situation that calls for delving into emotions, they are comfortable with helping others through the process. They may demand a lot of themselves as they attend to others' pain. They can be empathetic and humanitarian when they focus on others' suffering. However, when they consider their own suffering, they feel shame, which can lead to depression.

This particular Four can seem like a Seven because they do outlandish things, but instead of doing them for an adrenaline rush, it's their way to stand out. They can have a playful way about them but empathize with others who are grieving or sad in a way a Seven cannot.

The Social Four

Social Fours truly suffer in their minds and let everybody know it. They lament and wear their suffering on their sleeves. This Four becomes envious of relationships that they perceive others have. As they struggle with this envy, they make themselves the victim, lamenting and hoping that other people will help them. They compare themselves with others more than the other two subtypes of Fours, and they surmise how they are less than others. They look for ways in which they are lacking, which causes their self-image to fall even lower. They feel guilty for anything that they desire, thinking, "I shouldn't want this; I shouldn't need this; I shouldn't be envious of this." Because they do want those things, however, guilt and shame can become overwhelming. They appear sweet and soft-spoken while in public, but in private, they can become aggressive and mean. They still desire to stand out and be special but more often feel shame, loneliness, and hopelessness.

The encouraging side of this Four is that they can be very generous to others who are in need. Though they will not go out of their way to help others, when asked, they are willing to give generously to others in need.

The Sexual Four

This is the Four who makes others suffer. They project their suffering onto others, are competitive, and want to be the best. They do not think about being the best ethically or morally but want people to look up to them, to be seen as the best. They are not worried about being liked but want to be better than everybody else, usually minimizing other people's accomplishments so that they look better. They are usually arrogant and elitist. They want to be in the right crowd, right situations, and right relationship, according to how others see them. Any criticism or reproach is an affront to their character, and they don't put up with it well. Their envy comes out in anger. If you have heard the saying "Hurt people hurt people," it can certainly apply to this type. They are demanding, more aggressive, and angrier than the other two types of Fours.

Sexual Fours can be mistaken for an Eight because of their aggressive nature, but Fours show their anger more frequently than Eights. They can also look like the sexual Two, which means they can be very aggressive and seductive. However, the sexual Four is usually this way to show how good they are, not so that their needs will be met.

WHAT FOURS FEAR MOST

The Four's basic fear is having no identity or personal significance; therefore, their basic desire is to find them-selves and then find their significance. Knowing what they were created to do is a goal for them. Many believers strive to find the will of God for their lives. This is especially true for the Four. They want to know their purpose and what it is they were created for. As they learn to be in tune with the Spirit, they begin to understand that they were created to be in relationship with God, and as that relationship grows and develops, they can overcome feeling insignificant.

FOURS IN THE BIBLE

The writer of the book of Ecclesiastes had seen all things. He was rich, powerful, and possessed everything most people say brings happiness. But he was not happy. He wanted to find his purpose. "What a heavy burden God has laid on mankind! I have seen all the things that are done under the sun; all of them are meaningless, a chasing after the wind" (Eccl. 1:13–14). This sounds like a Four: looking for purpose and burdened by not knowing their significance in the world. It takes the whole book of Ecclesiastes for the writer to conclude that fulfillment does not come from the things we enjoy but from our relationship with the Almighty.

GROWTH FOR FOURS

But the fruit of the Spirit is love, joy, peace, patience,
kindness, goodness, faithfulness, gentleness,
self-control; against such things there is no law.
(Gal. 5:22–23 ESV)

The fruit of the Spirit is where growth starts for every number. For the Four, they naturally exhibit goodness as they work with others in their everyday lives, but their growth comes through the discovery that God brings out the goodness in them. They do not have to be good enough; they have to see themselves as God sees them—full of the goodness found in the outpouring of the Holy Spirit into their lives. "With this in mind, we constantly pray for you, that our God may make you worthy of his calling, and that by his power he may bring to fruition your every desire for goodness and your every deed prompted by faith" (2 Thess. 1:11).

I have seen Fours who are amazing people because they've gone through the growth process and know how to listen to the Holy Spirit, learn God's Word, and understand how God thinks about them. Fours need to understand that God created them as incredible, unique individuals who have a purpose in this life. The growth process requires them to notice how they respond and react to circumstances throughout their days.

As a Four, notice when you self-criticize, when you compare yourself to someone else, or when you are telling yourself negative beliefs. Then ask yourself, "Why am I focusing on those negative things?" Strive to take captive your thoughts. Ask the Lord to show you the good things about yourself: what you are good at, what your talents are, and how much God loves you. As you work through situations and relationships, notice when your focus shifts to what is missing. Pause to think what is good in that situation or relationship. Train yourself to look at not only what is missing but also what is present. Know that it is okay to sit in sadness and grief. Those emotions are part of who you are and allow you to relate to hurting people. However, you need to know how to come out of that grief and sadness and when to start moving forward.

Another growth point for the Four is to allow people to love you. Fours want so desperately to be loved, but feel as if they do not deserve it. When people are trying to show you love, you tend to throw up a barrier and pull away. Note when you do this and practice accepting love. As a Four, you do not want the pain of rejection, but allowing people into your life can bring a measure of joy and peace you have not been able to enjoy. To help you in these growth steps, here are some of the spiritual disciplines you may want to focus on.

THE SPIRITUAL DISCIPLINES
FOR FOURS

The disciplines that are easier for the type Four are solitude, silence, and prayer. Because Fours tend to be a little bit more introverted, solitude gives them that space to be alone with God, and they find a rhythm in that daily time. Being alone, still, and listening comforts Fours. A lot of types cannot sit in silence, but a Four can do that very well. As a practice in prayer or meditation, journaling seems to come a lot easier to the Fours than to other numbers. Not all Fours are great at journaling, but because they're creative and their minds work through the deep emotions, they can benefit from writing down their thoughts and prayers. If they use a creative process to express their thoughts, they can sit in prayer for quite some time. Because they easily connect with their emotions, the emotional struggle during prayer as they pour out their hearts to God can come naturally to them.

Challenging practices for the Four can be service, study, and worship. Service is others-focused and acting on what others need. The Four is naturally self-focused and, therefore, has a harder time identifying what other people need. They are not like Twos, who can see a need and fill it. Fours must actively seek ways to serve others.

Study can be a struggle for Fours because they like to focus on the emotional part of spiritual growth, not the intellectual. Taking time to study and dig deep intellectually is not exciting for the Four. The process of growth requires taking the Word of God and applying it to our lives. Studying the Word teaches us how God wants us to live and what he wants us to accomplish. That requires time and study, but the Four would rather read the Bible and think about how it makes them *feel*.

Worship can be easy when it is about feeling love toward God. But when it comes to finding joy and gratitude in who God is, the Four tends to lose ground. Gratitude and offering thanks to God for who he is and opening themselves up to experience the joy of God's presence can be hard when they are stuck in their melancholy.

The key thought to remember for the Four is, *God made me unique. I do not have to strive to stand out or be different. He gave his life so my joy might be complete. Remember to be grateful and enjoy the life God has for me.* And that is where the Four can grow. The key verse to remember is John 15:11: "I have told you this so that my joy may be in you and that your joy may be complete." Meditate on that verse and discover the joy and freedom you can have in Christ.

The world needs you, Fours. You are great at thinking outside the box. You can see solutions to problems that others cannot. Quit trying to be unique. Enjoy the beauty in the mundane and know that you make the world a more interesting place just by being you.

QUESTIONS FOR A FOUR

1. What good things are happening in my life right now?

2. How do I feel loved by others?

3. How do I push people away who are trying to show me love?

4. When do I allow criticism to play over and over in my head?

5. When do I use hopelessness or depression to avoid making something positive happen?

6. What are my strengths? What am I good at?

7. What makes my closest relationship good?

8. How am I able to use my gift of emotional connection to help those around me? How do I get stuck in thinking about myself?

QUESTIONS FOR THOSE WHO WORK OR LIVE WITH A FOUR

1. How can I be open to sharing my feelings with the Four and not always focus on logical conversation?

2. How do I encourage them to share their thoughts and feelings?

3. Do I take the time to frame negative feedback within the thought of growth opportunities?

4. How can I be authentic and open with a Four?

5. How am I able to allow them to be creative and expressive in our relationship?

VERSES FOR MEDITATION FOR FOURS

The Lord said, "Go out and stand on the mountain in the presence of the Lord, for the Lord is about to pass by." Then a great and powerful wind tore the mountains apart and shattered the rocks before the Lord, but the Lord was not in the wind. After the wind there was an earthquake, but the Lord was not in the earthquake. After the earthquake came a fire, but the Lord was not in the fire. And after the fire came a gentle whisper. When Elijah heard it, he pulled his cloak over his face and went out and stood at the mouth of the cave.

1 Kings 19:11–13

· · · · ·

JOB

The book of Job shows how Job worked through the knowledge he had of his love for God as well as the emotions he was working through with his friends and the circumstances around him. Through it all, he never questioned God's sovereignty and power over all.

Psalm 27:7–9

．　．　．　．　．

Hear my voice when I call, LORD; be merciful to me and answer me. My heart says of you, "Seek his face!" Your face, LORD, I will seek. Do not hide your face from me, do not turn your servant away in anger; you have been my helper. Do not reject me or forsake me, God my Savior.

For you created my inmost being; you knit me together in my mother's womb. I praise you because I am fearfully and wonderfully made; your works are wonderful, I know that full well.

Psalm 139:13–14

．　．　．　．　．

Unity and Diversity in the Body of Christ
1 Corinthians 12:12–30

．　．　．　．　．

Rejoice in the Lord always. I will say it again: Rejoice!
Philippians 4:4

．　．　．　．　．

TYPE FIVE

THE INVESTIGATOR

Fear: Being useless, incapable, and depleted
Verse to Memorize: Come now, let us reason together, says the LORD: though your sins are like scarlet, they shall be as white as snow; though they are red like crimson, they shall become like wool. (Isa. 1:18 ESV)

TYPE FIVE OVERVIEW

Type Five is known as the Investigator. This type begins the Head (thinking) triad along with the Six and Seven. The passion for the Five is avarice or greed. It's not materialistic greed but greed for knowledge and to be the one who possesses the information. It is also the greed of not wanting to give away anything they have in case it cannot be replaced, for they do not want to be without. That applies to possessions, energy, and emotions.

They're factual, intellectual people. If you ask a Five what he *feels*, he will tell you what he *thinks*. They can lack empathy for others' emotional struggles, because they avoid their own emotions and use rational thought to get through their struggles.

They mostly live in their heads and rely on thinking and acquiring knowledge. They need evidence-based decision-making, and they can argue a case logically but typically lack the emotional response necessary to create intimate relationships. They are not usually in the spotlight and are dedicated to making sure things are done correctly. They make great engineers, lawyers, and professors. When they do appear to be engaging and extroverted, they are with people who think the same way they do. Someone with whom they can have an intellectual conversation brings them to life.

Fives use their resources economically so that they don't have to depend on anything external. When they have what they need, they won't have external demands that others can limit or control. Therefore, they try to minimize needs as much as possible. Their internal support comes through information. A Five thrives on information and boundaries, from which they get their security.

Fives need time alone to rest and recharge and are usually introverts. They observe people in situations rather than participate in what's going on. They avoid their emotions because it drains their energy store. They are analytical and can logically look at situations and be rational whereas most of the other types rely on emotion to guide them. They are calm in a crisis and think through problems before reacting. They value boundaries and respect other people's boundaries. They can hold confidences and become loyal friends to a few. Long before a social interaction occurs, they spend mental energy thinking through how the situation should go and what should take place. This is why social interaction is exhausting to them.

Fives enjoy organization and classification, which they do in most every area of their lives. To connect with others, they share their knowledge. Finding someone who is interested in or has expertise in the same interests creates energy and connection for the Five.

THE THREE SUBTYPES OF FIVES

The three subtypes in the type Five are all very similar, making the subtypes difficult to figure out. Motivation is the key to discovering how they fit into this type.

The Self-Preservation Five

The self-preservation Five is the most "Five-ish" in that their outward appearances and motivations align. They maintain boundaries, want a place to go where nobody can bother them, and usually erect thick walls to protect themselves from connecting with others. They view the world as hostile, so they tend to avoid communicating with others even more than the other Five types. They are minimalistic and try not to have many needs or wants. They minimize their lifestyles so they can avoid being dependent on other people. They try to adapt in social settings to fit in so that they don't stand out.

The Social Five

This Five subtype has an ideal or ultimate meaning in life to guide them. They want to relate to people who share their intellect and interests. They appear aloof to others in the group they hang around with because they relate mainly to ideas and knowledge. They are looking for connections with people who are at the top of the game in their area of interest. They want to connect with those who are the highest in that intellect, so they limit who they want in their circle. They want to be somebody important in those people's eyes, but they would never admit it.

Spiritually, they can become biblically minded, but these Fives take what's called a "spiritual bypass." They want all the intellect and see the ultimate goal of spirituality, but they avoid doing the emotional and psychological work that it takes to grow as a Christian. These Fives understand eternal life and the goal of the Christian, but they don't allow the relationship to happen, because it involves their emotional being as well as their mental being.

The Sexual Five

This is the counter type of the type Five. They have a very romantic ideal of what a relationship should look like. They seek experiences with that one person who is worthy, can be trusted, and meets their romantic ideal. They are easily disappointed if those relationships don't meet that ideal. This applies to romantic relationships, friendships, and even mentors and coaches. This Five is more in tune with feelings, which can be intense. They can sometimes resemble a Four because they have that romantic side, but they use their intellect to process their emotions.

Trust is the basic issue in relationships. They need somebody to be open and honest with them and who allows them to be open and honest. They must be able to trust that other person with their emotions. They have a connection with their feelings more than other Fives, but they don't let them show unless they connect with their romantic side. There is a constant struggle between withdrawing and withholding versus the need to connect with and trust someone.

WHAT FIVES FEAR MOST

Because the Five's value is based on intellectual knowledge, their inner fear is being useless, unable to function in a situation, or unable to answer questions asked of them. They do not want to look like they don't know what they're talking about, and they won't take part in a conversation about a topic they're not familiar with. They fear being overwhelmed by emotions or demands of others. This can cause them to go inward and withdraw into a world of words and research. They also fear being depleted, which especially applies to their energy. They tend to hoard it to protect the little they believe they have. To give any of it away would mean having even less when needed.

Fives need to unbind their emotions to truly understand what the Holy Spirit wants to do with them. The Spirit of God works in ways that do not always use logic and understanding. Faith and love are emotional steps taken when logic has exhausted itself. We can see God in a logical way, but the relationship God wants with us takes us to a new level. The fruit of the Spirit that helps a Five do that is love, an emotional response to a logical sequence of events. The logical part of a Five can study the Bible, research the life of Christ, and see how much God loves. The emotional response to accept that love and strive to be in a close, life-changing relationship is the hardest response for a Five. Fives can spend their whole lives learning about God, the church, and the Bible but remain disconnected emotionally. That is not what God intended. You will see this more as we look at the Bible character for this number.

FIVES IN THE BIBLE

Nicodemus was a Pharisee and a member of the Sanhedrin. He was a top Jewish leader and lawyer in his time. He is mentioned three times in the book of John, and we see tremendous growth in his life in the little mentioned about him.

Nicodemus first came to Jesus at night to ask a question. Some scholars think he came at night to avoid being seen. Others say he came at night so that he could have

Jesus to himself—a one-on-one conversation instead of in front of crowds of people. His statements were factual and grounded as he talked with Jesus. He saw the evidence of the miracles Jesus had performed and came to a logical conclusion about who Jesus is: "He came to Jesus at night and said, 'Rabbi, we know that you are a teacher who has come from God. For no one could perform the signs you are doing if God were not with him'" (John 3:2). Jesus then forced Nicodemus to think outside of logic. Nicodemus wanted to find the answers, but he couldn't get out of his head. Jesus' talk with him must have made him think about his responses and his expectation of faith because the next time we see Nicodemus, he was defending Jesus before his fellow Pharisees. The last time we see him, it is evident a change had occurred in his life. He was with Joseph of Arimathea at the burial of Jesus. Nicodemus brought the myrrh and aloes to anoint Jesus' body. This would have been an expensive gesture. When a Five becomes generous, he moves out of his head and logic, sees others' needs, and gives out of his abundance.

GROWTH FOR FIVES

But the fruit of the Spirit is love, joy, peace, patience,
kindness, goodness, faithfulness, gentleness,
self-control; against such things there is no law.
(Gal. 5:22–23 ESV)

The fruit of the Spirit is where growth starts for every number. For Fives, they naturally exhibit patience as they study and learn. However, that patience is gone if they ever feel they do not know something or feel someone is trying to deplete them. As they discover the patience of God through the power of the Holy Spirit, they can share their knowledge with those who need to understand. Their focus can change from holding on to everything they have to freely giving to those in need. "Preach the word; be prepared in season and out of season; correct, rebuke and encourage—with great patience and careful instruction" (2 Tim. 4:2).

How can the Five grow? Satan's lies resonate with Fives. The lie of scarcity is a big one. The Word of God tells us that he wants us to have abundant lives. Satan wants us to believe that our resources are limited. Whether that is limited time, space, energy, or material things, our response is to challenge those lies with the Word of God. Do I really have a lack of resources, or is that a false belief? Studying Scripture will show Fives that the more they hold on to their resources—whether it is time, energy, money, or knowledge—the less blessing they receive from our Father. Fives can learn to be generous with their time, energy, and resources. This will challenge their sense of security and help them become aware that we are truly secure only in Christ.

Fives can also strive to become aware of when they cut off an emotion. It is such an unconscious response that it may take some time to notice when they do it. The reaction of always going to the head when they are in a situation and not even considering the emotional aspect of a problem is automatic. To be willing to open themselves to the emotional aspect of the solution is a growth point for them, as well as allowing themselves to experience anger, sadness, fear, or joy. Rather than push away emotion, Fives do well to let themselves feel that emotion in their bodies.

Take note if you have excessive boundaries with the people in your life that hold you back from enjoying a life-enriching connection. Notice how you ration your energy. Do you really have limited energy, or have you trained yourself to believe it? Evaluate if you are tired and drained at the end of the day, or if you could do more with your time and energy.

Observe people in your life instead of looking to the ideal of what life should be like. When you focus on an ideal, it can lead you into depression because the world doesn't match up. For the romantic Five, notice when the standards in your relationships are not realistic, remembering that relationships are never perfect. They require work, effort, and love. Celebrate the small victories. When you can, connect with your emotions, be generous, allow people to make mistakes, and allow yourself to not know something. Celebrate those victories and keep moving forward.

Another way for the Five to grow is to exercise. Because Fives often withdraw into their minds when stressed, getting out of the head and doing something with the body is a great way to balance the Five. Go for a walk or run. Dance around the room. Exercise can make you sharper and give you more internal resources to accomplish your work. To help you in these growth steps, the following are some of the spiritual disciplines you may want to focus on.

THE SPIRITUAL DISCIPLINES
FOR FIVES

As we get into the spiritual disciplines, study, solitude, and simplicity may come easy for Fives. These are all basic attributes of the Five's character. They love research and developing their minds. The challenge comes when they focus on learning but don't share what they've learned. Sharing the things that God is showing from Scripture and being willing to teach others is a great step of faith for the Five. It also requires energy to teach, and the Five will need to learn to give some of that away. They will find that God increases their sense of stored energy as they use it to bring out God's glory.

Fives can practice solitude, because they protect them-selves when alone. They like to spend that time alone in research and study. However, one of the hard things that solitude requires is listening to what God wants them to hear. Turning off the research and knowledge part of their brains to listen to the Holy Spirit and grow in relationship with God can be challenging.

Simplicity can also be easy for Fives. They fear being depleted, so they tend to keep the minimal possessions needed to survive and don't strive for more. They like to minimize their needs and use resources economically so they can control external demands. However, the practice of simplicity for the Five is to rely on God for necessities, and not always try to control their provisions. God is our great provider, and as we give generously, he replenishes what we need.

More difficult for Fives may be confession and service. Confession, because they don't like to interact with people on such a personal level but prefer an intellectual level. Interacting with people on an emotional level drains them. Also, sharing sin in their lives or the temptations they struggle with requires an emotional connection that scares Fives, leaving them feeling vulnerable and unsafe. Learning to trust another person with this part of themselves and understanding that confession is necessary for their faith journey are additional challenges. They would do well to accept that struggle does not make them a lesser person, neither do faults nor challenges make them inferior. Rather, these common characteristics make them human.

Service for the Five can be another difficult practice because they like the safety of intellect versus the strain of social and emotional life. Service requires an emotional connection, a willingness to see and respond to the needs around them—to give of themselves to help others. They have to trust God that it is not an option for the Christian to stay safe by isolating themselves. God requires us to serve others out of the outpouring of his love in us and then letting it flow through us into others. Living a more generous life of service is vital for their—and all types'—spiritual health and journey.

A key verse for the Five is, "But those who hope in the LORD will renew their strength. They will soar on wings like eagles; they will run and not grow weary, they will walk and not be faint" (Isa. 40:31). The key thought for the Five is, *My safety and security come through Christ. I can open up to others so that Christ can be known by others knowing me.* The Five has a wealth of knowledge and understanding of Scripture to share with others. If you're a Five, as you study God's Word, pray for God to bring you opportunities to share your knowledge and understanding with others so that they, too, can know Christ.

The world needs you. When you are spiritually healthy, you become generous with your resources. You give out of your abundance, from your wealth of knowledge, and are among the greatest humanitarians in the world.

QUESTIONS FOR A FIVE

1. What kinds of situations make me want to move into my head? What pulls me away from the situation? How can I stay present?

2. How am I pulling away from someone or something that stirs my emotions?

3. What emotions am I comfortable with?

4. What emotions am I not comfortable with?

5. When do I feel I don't have enough time? Energy? Resources? How do I respond?

6. How do I appreciate others around me? How do I let them know?

7. When do I share my knowledge with those who need it?

QUESTIONS FOR THOSE WHO WORK OR LIVE WITH A FIVE

1. How can I better express my thoughts clearly and logically?

2. How can I give them time and space to think through situations?

3. How can I be honest and straightforward about what I see and feel?

4. How can I draw them into conversations?

5. When am I able to notice when they are withdrawn or shutting down?

VERSES FOR MEDITATION FOR FIVES

You, God, are awesome in your sanctuary;
the God of Israel gives power and strength
to his people. Praise be to God!
Psalm 68:35

. . . . .

A friend loves at all times,
and a brother is born for a time of adversity.
Proverbs 17:17

. . . . .

As iron sharpens iron, so one person sharpens another.
Proverbs 27:17

. . . . .

But those who hope in the Lord will renew their strength.
They will soar on wings like eagles; they will run and
not grow weary, they will walk and not be faint.
Isaiah 40:31

. . . . .

The thief comes only to steal and kill and destroy; I have
come that they may have life, and have it to the full.

John 10:10

. . . . .

So in Christ we, though many, form one body,
and each member belongs to all the others.

Romans 12:5

. . . . .

Carry each other's burdens, and in this way
you will fulfill the law of Christ.

Galatians 6:2

. . . . .

My God will meet all your needs according
to the riches of his glory in Christ Jesus.

Philippians 4:19

. . . . .

Therefore confess your sins to each other and pray
for each other so that you may be healed. The prayer
of a righteous person is powerful and effective.

James 5:16

. . . . .

TYPE SIX

THE LOYALIST

Fear: Not being safe/secure
Verse to Memorize: He will cover you with his feathers, and under his wings you will find refuge; his faithfulness will be your shield and rampart. (Ps. 91:4)

TYPE SIX OVERVIEW

The second type in the Head triad, with Five and Seven, is Six. Known as the Loyalist, Sixes tend to be extremely loyal to their friends. They don't ever want to be abandoned or left without support; therefore, to have that security and support to fulfill their basic desire, the Six offers loyalty to others.

Sixes believe they don't possess the internal resources to handle life's challenges on their own, so they increasingly rely on structures and support outside of themselves for guidance to survive. Their passion is fear. They live in their heads and tend to let their thoughts run away, creating fear and anxiety. They don't have confidence in their judgments or listen to their inner guidance, so they seek it from other people. They are reliable and hard-working, excellent troubleshooters, and able to foresee problems. However, they can be anxious and suspicious.

Sixes struggle to trust others, themselves, and authority. They seek security and support and continually scan for danger. Depending on their subtype, they manage what they perceive as fear or anxiety through either fight or flight. All the subtypes of Six fear letting down their defenses, so they hide what they are thinking. They can appear hard and aggressive as a way of hiding their fears from others. Also, sometimes they don't understand their fears, so they cannot articulate the cause of their anxiety.

Sixes are some of the most loyal friends you may ever have. Building trust with Sixes takes time and effort; however, once it is built, they are loyal to the end.

Sixes are excellent troubleshooters and problem solvers. They can see what could go wrong and usually find ways to prevent those occurrences. They can be calm in a crisis, because they've already thought through possibilities and how to manage them. This allows them to be clear-headed.

Sixes are intuitive and read people well, seeing through pretenses or masks people wear. They find hidden agendas easily. Therefore, they are wary and skeptical of authority figures. They look for authentic people.

THE THREE SUBTYPES OF SIXES

Like the other types, there are three subtypes of Sixes.

The Self-Preservation Six

This Six is the quietest and most kind-hearted. When dealing with authority figures, they quietly avoid them. In other words, they try not to deal with them, because they don't trust them. Their fears initiate insecurity, making them depend on other people for security. Their friendships create the security they need. They hold on to people they trust and depend on them to create a safe environment. These Sixes feel fear the most.

As friends, self-preservation Sixes are trustworthy and supportive. They are not confident in defending their self-interests or providing for their own needs, again depending on their friends. This dependence creates a fear of disappointing those closest to them.

These Sixes hide their emotions of anger and fear to avoid confrontation. They have a hard time making decisions because they doubt themselves. They are intelligent and can see several options and discuss them, but they struggle to make a final decision and instead allow others to decide for them.

The Social Six

Social Sixes are the competitive Sixes. They are rebellious against authority figures and look for hidden agendas. They have a general sense of distrust until they find an authority figure they can look up to. Once they find that person, they may become fanatically devoted to them. Fear of that person's disapproval drives what they do.

Social Sixes are the opposite of self-preservation Sixes in that they are intolerant of indecision. They want to decide but are not spontaneous about it. They think through their options.

These Sixes tend to see the world as black and white and seem to easily discern the course they should take. They may appear to deliberate, because they do not want to disappoint their leaders or do something the wrong way and get into trouble. They can appear to be a One on the outside because they strive to do the right thing; but again, it comes down to motivation. The One wants to do what is right out of their sense of right and wrong, while a Six wants to do what is right to please those in authority over them.

The Sexual Six

The sexual Six is the counter type. They are suspicious of authority figures, and when confrontation happens, they put on a powerful front. This subtype does not like to admit to their fear; they shift into fight mode when confronting it. When feeling threatened, sexual Sixes strive to appear more powerful to keep the enemy away. To overcome their fear of appearing weak, they use intimidation. In fact, they move toward danger instead of avoiding it. These reactions to fear come from the idea that fear should be eliminated and that they shouldn't have this feeling. So, they work to become powerful to overcome it. Therefore, they come across as impressive to others.

WHAT SIXES FEAR MOST

Many stories in the Bible talk about being afraid—such as the army that faced Goliath every day; David as he fled from Saul; and the disciples in the boat when the storm arose. Those were real threats, and our human nature is to fear what can hurt us. But the fear I am referring to is the fear of a perceived or imagined danger, to live in a perpetual state of fearing what disaster *might* happen. Always looking for what could go wrong and looking for ways to protect themselves if this or that happens is part of a Six's everyday life, along with worry and anxiety. It is a hard way to live, but the good thing is that the world needs Sixes—to be aware of the possibilities and to be prepared for what could happen. However, to live in that state all the time takes a toll on Sixes' physical and spiritual well-being. It can feel paralyzing to do what God is asking of them because of what could happen.

It takes Sixes time to trust people, but when they do, they are extremely loyal and are most faithful friends. Allowing the Spirit to use their gift of seeing the world this way for the good of all is their growth point. To learn to live a life of peace and joy through the power of God is an amazing journey for the Six.

One example of the struggle many Sixes face is when they are asked to make decisions in a group setting. As the group goes through the process, the Six is insecure in their ideas and unwilling to speak up, but impatient when nothing is being done. When they see nothing is being accomplished, they become direct and somewhat aggressive in finally sharing their idea. Many Sixes have expressed that they walk a fine line between being a pushover and being overly aggressive. Sixes who are aware of their internal conversations and how they build toward aggression can begin to see when they cross the line of being too aggressive or when they actually do need to speak out.

SIXES IN THE BIBLE

Two Bible characters who stand out to me as demonstrating fear versus faithfulness are Ruth and Peter. Ruth had much to feel insecure about while adopting her new culture. Her husband had died, and her mother-in-law was a widow as well. Food and security were supposed to come from the family unit, but it was in another country. Her loyalty to Naomi was unquestionable, and her willingness to go with her—away from the security of her own family— was a difficult choice. When Ruth arrived in Israel, she had to surrender herself to a stranger for food and security. Naomi's faith in God was evident to Ruth, who trusted in the God of Naomi to take care of her. She had much to fear and feel insecure about, but in the face of it, she found a way to be loyal and courageous to accomplish the task at hand. She did not allow her problems to paralyze her, but instead, reminded herself of God's security and faithfulness to get her through.

Peter is a great example of two different ways to respond to fear: fight or flight. In some cases, he fought when he was faced with a problem. Cutting off the ear of the high priest's servant was a fight reaction to his threatened security. But when asked to stand by Jesus in the courtyard after Jesus was arrested, he chose the flight mode. He was always aware of the fear within him, but he learned that fear did not need to make him ineffective; rather, he could submit his fears to God, who turned them into powerful tools for him. God's faithfulness never lets us down and will turn our fears into courage.

GROWTH FOR SIXES

But the fruit of the Spirit is love, joy, peace, patience,
kindness, goodness, faithfulness, gentleness,
self-control; against such things there is no law.
(Gal. 5:22–23 ESV)

The fruit of the Spirit is where growth starts for every number. Sixes naturally exhibit faithfulness in their everyday lives, but their growth comes through the discovery that the faithfulness of God is their security. "May the God of hope fill you with all joy and peace as you trust in him, so that you may overflow with hope by the power of the Holy Spirit" (Rom. 15:13).

If you are a Six, remember that there are uncertainties in life no matter how much you prepare. Our faith in God comes when we rely on the Holy Spirit to guide and direct us. Also, we tend to find what we look for. Have you ever purchased a new car and then seen that kind of car everywhere? You never noticed it before, but now that you own one, you look for others like it. The same is true in life. If we look for those things that can threaten our security, we're going to find them. But if we focus on where we are secure, we find the peace we seek.

Sixes also feel pressured for time when they are overwhelmed and overthinking circumstances. They can become impatient, delegate less, and begin to second-guess things they have been preparing for. Their internal narrative begins to bring out their insecurity, and they become overwhelmed. When this happens, begin by acknowledging the boundaries of the situation. Be aware of what is feasible and what is not. Make your choices manageable and be willing to be receptive about what others are saying and doing. Take time to allow the Holy Spirit to change the narrative inside and create a more secure place where you are free to be creative and listen to those around you.

Another way for the Six to grow is through physical exercise. It helps you to get out of your head and into your body. Taking a brisk walk, doing twenty-five jumping jacks, or anything that gets your body focused for a bit can get you out of the internal narrative of insecurity and bring you to a place where the Holy Spirit can start showing you what is actually helpful in a situation and what is just something you believe to be helpful.

Meditation and reading the Word of God allow you to thoughtfully consider your fears. Are these fears real, or are they imagined or perceived fears? Learn the difference between real danger, potential danger, and hypothetical danger. Our bodies respond to all in the same way. We need to be sure we are sending the correct information to our bodies, so the response is appropriate. If we are constantly in flight or fight mode, our bodies suffer. When you experience fear, consider where the fear is coming from and if it is real or not. Articulating the fear will help you work through it. Chances are that you'll realize the fear is in your head and not real.

It is okay to go a little crazy and have some fun. Let your guard down and enjoy life. It will be easiest to do with those you trust and are comfortable with. Listen to your instincts. Though you are a thinker, allow yourself to listen to instinct rather than logic sometimes.

Remember that you have something to offer the world. You just need the confidence in who you are and what you can do to give back to those around you. Also, learn how to be more vulnerable. Don't be so strict and controlling of your emotions. Understand that real strength and courage come from tapping into that vulnerability. Some of the strongest leaders are not the powerhouses but those who are real with the people following them. Again, let your guard down and find a way to feel the pleasure of a moment. To help you in these growth steps here are some of the spiritual disciplines you may want to focus on.

THE SPIRITUAL DISCIPLINES
FOR SIXES

As we look at the Six's spiritual disciplines, meditation and worship may come naturally. In worship, singing and journaling are grounding exercises that will help the Six place their awe of God in the forefront of their thinking. It's a way to express their faith in the face of their fears and helps to solidify the truth that in Christ they are safe. Recognizing how amazing God's love is for them and his ability to be their provider fulfills their need for security. God doesn't want them to live in fear but in the freedom of Christ, so journaling—getting their fears and thoughts written out—is a positive way for the Six to worship.

Meditating on God's Word helps Sixes' minds focus on how God wants to overcome their fears. It encourages them to slow down and face their fears with God, who loves them. The Word of God also helps them understand how his love is revealed through struggles and that his wisdom will lead them through the fears. Journaling comes in handy in the meditation process as well. Writing out what they hear from God helps them overcome the doubts and mistrust they may be facing.

The practices that may be harder for the Six are studying and fasting. Because the Six is in the Head triad, you might think that studying would be easy for them, but it challenges their anxious, busy minds. It requires discipline and focus. However, when practiced, it can help anchor them. If they're willing to be disciplined in the study of God's

Word and internalize Scripture, they can call on those truths for courage whenever they face anxiety or fear. Memorizing Scripture is a great way for Sixes to help them take captive every thought.

Fasting helps to ground them into the reality that God wants them to live consciously aware of his presence instead of focusing on problems and challenges. It awakens their hunger for God and helps them realize that God wants to meet their deepest needs. They learn not to look outside of their relationship with Christ to have their needs met. The Holy Spirit wants to take away the anxiety, fear, and mistrust and replace it with joy, peace, and courage, along with the capacity to trust God deeply.

A key verse for the Six is Joshua 1:9: "Have I not commanded you? Be strong and courageous. Do not be afraid; do not be discouraged, for the LORD your God will be with you wherever you go." The key thought for the Six is, *I can bring my fears and insecurities to God because he is my refuge and strength. He will give me courage and confidence because he cares about me.*

Sixes, remember that you are stronger and more capable than you think. Your leadership, loyalty, commitment, and even your questions are highly valued. Just like Peter, you are the rock of the church. You keep us connected and secure. We need you.

QUESTIONS FOR A SIX

1. When do I trust myself to make good decisions?

2. When do I look for everything that can go wrong?

3. How do I focus on the possibilities more than the reality?

4. Whom do I trust most? How do I make decisions that are based on not letting them down?

5. How am I able to use both logic and intuition to face situations?

6. What is going well in my life right now?

7. What decisions must I make right now? Am I waiting for someone else to decide for me?

8. What are ways I can offer help or care to someone?

QUESTIONS FOR THOSE WHO WORK OR LIVE WITH A SIX

1. How can I make them feel safe and let them know I am a trustworthy friend?

2. How can I be supportive and encouraging when they are making a decision?

3. How can I gently give constructive criticism?

4. When expressing myself, how can I be calm and logical without creating drama?

VERSES FOR MEDITATION FOR SIXES

Be strong and courageous. Do not be afraid or
terrified because of them, for the Lord your God goes
with you; he will never leave you nor forsake you.

Deuteronomy 31:6

· · · · ·

Have I not commanded you? Be strong and courageous.
Do not be afraid; do not be discouraged, for the Lord
your God will be with you wherever you go.

Joshua 1:9

· · · · ·

When anxiety was great within me,
your consolation brought me joy.

Psalm 94:19

· · · · ·

Trust in the Lord with all your heart and lean not
on your own understanding; in all your ways
submit to him, and he will make your paths straight.

Proverbs 3:5–6

· · · · ·

And surely I am with you always, to the
very end of the age.
Matthew 28:20

. . . . .

Therefore I tell you, do not worry about your life, what you
will eat or drink; or about your body, what you will wear. Is
not life more than food, and the body more than clothes?
Look at the birds of the air; they do not sow or reap or
store away in barns, and yet your heavenly Father feeds
them. Are you not much more valuable than they? Can any
one of you by worrying add a single hour to your life?
Matthew 6:25–27

. . . . .

For I am convinced that neither death nor life, neither
angels nor demons, neither the present nor the future,
nor any powers, neither height nor depth, nor anything
else in all creation, will be able to separate us from
the love of God that is in Christ Jesus our Lord.
Romans 8:38–39

. . . . .

TYPE SEVEN

THE ENTHUSIAST

Fear: Being deprived or in pain

Verses to Memorize: For those who live according to the flesh set their minds on the things of the flesh, but those who live according to the Spirit set their minds on the things of the Spirit. For to set the mind on the flesh is death, but to set the mind on the Spirit is life and peace. (Rom. 8:5–6 ESV)

TYPE SEVEN OVERVIEW

The last number in the Head triad, with the Five and the Six, is the Seven, known as the Enthusiast. Sevens' passion is gluttony. We often think of food when we talk about that passion, but gluttony is more than food for the Seven; it is wanting to fill their emptiness with things and experiences—pleasures. Their gluttony is more about that next great experience or collecting more things that make them feel safe. They are all about fun and excitement.

Sevens are probably the most upbeat, extroverted type in the Enneagram. They appear to be full of heart but actually operate from their heads. They think through their lives so that each day promises as much fun and as little pain as possible. They have a hard time being in the moment, because they're always thinking about the next thing. They focus on the light and bright side of life, putting a positive or optimistic spin on everything and avoiding pain at all costs. In doing this, they seek to change their memories to block out the negative. They are busy, seek variety, and thrive on spontaneity. They can be versatile but scattered.

Sevens' core emotion is fear, but instead of thinking about the fear or finding ways to confront the fear, they try to move away from it. They are self-referencing, which means their worldview is based on what their needs are and what can get them to the next great thing.

Because they are in the Head triad, Sevens enjoy activities that stimulate the mind. And they like getting their minds involved in whatever they're doing. Their minds move very quickly from one idea to another. If you've ever worked on a team with a Seven, you know they are very good at brainstorming.

Sevens like to be challenged and are good at learning new things. They like taking in information and synthesizing it. They can be all over the place, because so many thoughts run through their minds, which is where the scatteredness comes in—jumping from idea to idea, often leaving other people behind. They tend to have excellent eye-hand coordination, which aids in learning new skills quickly. This can frustrate others who have put in years of practice, only to be outdone by a Seven who just started. However, Sevens do not have confidence in their abilities, because they learned them so quickly. It seems too easy, so they must not be doing it right. There is a juxtaposition of being excellent at something and not knowing it, because they didn't feel like they worked for it.

Sevens are not confident at making decisions, especially in relationships. They want what is best for the relationship but have a hard time determining what is best. So instead of making a decision, they move on to the next thing and leave that decision behind. When they consider their options, they become overwhelmed. They don't take the time to narrow their choices to one or two. They prefer the trial-and-error method, because they like to try new things. If one option doesn't work, they'll try something else. If that doesn't work, they'll move on to something else. That process can be frustrating for those they are working with or in relationships with.

Sometimes, Sevens are called the eternal child because they don't want to grow up and take on the responsibility and commitment adulting requires. Some of the subtypes especially fall into this. They want to focus on the bright side of everything, being overly optimistic in seeing only the best in everybody and every situation, while often overlooking the negative. They can miss potential problems and oftentimes move forward without the benefit of critical thinking. They can ignore information that doesn't fit their positive outlook.

THE THREE SUBTYPES OF SEVENS

Like all the other subtypes, there are three subtypes of Sevens.

The Self-Preservation Seven

The self-preservation Seven likes to pull people in as a community so that they have everything they need. They are great at making networks and connections because they can reach out and talk with anyone. They are always looking for a good deal. They could be the lady to whom you say, "I love your purse," and excitedly responds, "Oh my gosh. I got it at the store, and it was, like, 90 percent off." She goes into great detail about her marvelous find.

Sevens' gluttony comes out in consumerism. They want more than they need: shopping, spending, and accumulating. They tend to confuse desires and needs. They panic if they feel like they are scarce in anything, and then over buy. They want to make sure they're not ever dependent on somebody else, and they don't want other people dependent on them. They want to be self-sufficient and know that they have enough; thus, they can be materialistic.

The Social Seven

This is the counter type of the Sevens. Their passion is gluttony, but they feel a sense of shame in it. Therefore, they go to the extreme of anti-gluttony. They try to avoid looking like they want more, so they develop their ideal picture of the world and themselves. They want to be a better person—to be pure and great in the eyes of others.

These Sevens worry a lot about their health, making sure that they're doing the best to take care of their bodies. They can view one aspect of their lives and be anti-glutton in that area. This is seen in the way they eat or maybe the way that they exercise. They also live simpler lives than the consumer Sevens and get by on less to prove their goodness.

They like to have possessions but don't want to appear that they have them. They take stock of themselves to make sure that they're not doing too much to look good in the eyes of others. Yet they look for recognition and adoration and want to be noticed for their sacrifices. They experience some guilt and shame, because of their gluttony tendencies, which can lead them to increase their anti-gluttony actions. They are enthusiastic, have good social skills, and can help with vision setting.

The Sexual Seven

Out of all of the sexual subtypes we have covered, the sexual Seven is the least about sex. They are dreamers who love the idea of love, but it's not necessarily a sexual drive for them. Their gluttony is not lust in the sexual aspect; it's lust for that perfect relationship. They can be somewhat naïve because they don't understand the reality of relationships. They live in a world of their imagined perfection.

They are not interested in the boring and routine: laundry, dishes, and mundane tasks are so "yuck." They want to live in a higher world, in a better reality, so their heads are in the clouds. They embellish reality and make it better than what it is. Reframing is part of their thinking process. For example, when they talk about their houses, they embellish it to be better than what it actually is.

These Sevens are lighthearted and enjoy life. They avoid anything boring, as well as painful, even avoiding talking about pain, suffering, or fear. They are trusting, seeing people in an idealistic view. They love to talk, so they can talk your ear off. They love to improvise and be the one who comes up with a solution. They find satisfaction in not missing anything, so they fear missing out. They want to consume as many experiences as they can. For example, if they have a three-day vacation with the possibility of ten activities, rather than narrow their choices to a few, these Sevens will find a way to do all ten, whatever it takes, because that's the ideal.

WHAT SEVENS FEAR MOST

The Seven's basic fear is being deprived or being in pain; therefore, their basic desire is to be satisfied and content. They use stimulation and an adrenaline rush to distract themselves from any pain or inner discomfort. The Seven does not appear to have fear and anxiety. They use their intellect to dismiss what they perceive as a difficult emotion. They think at a fast pace and can usually quickly move past painful or "negative" emotions in their thought lives. They fear having to work through a difficult emotion and deal with their failures, believing that if they move on to something more exciting and enticing, the negative emotion or stress disappears.

Another fear for Sevens is getting stuck in the painful feeling they are trying to work through. This fear motivates them to focus on the positive and strive to keep their emotions in a happy, safe place. Most Sevens do this subconsciously, not realizing that they rationalize away fears and use fun and exciting situations to forget the fear. Their thought lives subconsciously create paths to avoid anything that becomes unpleasant or uncomfortable.

SEVENS IN THE BIBLE

I chose King David as an example of a Seven. Again, I can only look at what we know from Scripture and cannot presume to know his motivations, but as we look at his life, I observe many Seven moments. He excelled at many skills. He fought off lions and bears as a shepherd boy. He made the rash decision to fight a giant with only a sling—and won. He was an excellent musician and writer. However, he also had moments of gluttony that landed him in trouble with God. Wanting more than the women he already had, he summoned Bathsheba, whom he saw from his roof. Taking what he desired, he seemed to look for the next thing to conquer. He danced, full of joy (and nearly naked), before the Lord. He lived to the fullest, sometimes without regard to the Lord. But he always found his way back to God. He seemed willing to work through his emotions, which is why, I believe he stayed connected with God.

GROWTH FOR SEVENS

But the fruit of the Spirit is love, joy, peace, patience,
kindness, goodness, faithfulness, gentleness,
self-control; against such things there is no law.
(Gal. 5:22–23 ESV)

The fruit of the Spirit is where growth starts for every number. Sevens naturally exhibit joy in every area of their lives. They love life and it shows. However, their joy is only as deep as the next experience. As they allow the Holy Spirit to fill them, they discover that joy cannot be taken away. Joy is so much more than happiness. When it's grounded in God, it can be found even in pain and failure. "I have told you this so that my joy may be in you and that your joy may be complete" (John 15:11).

Sevens will grow from their mistakes and hurts if they allow themselves. They don't experience growth unless they engage more deeply with their emotions—learning that pain, anxiety, and fear are part of life. Rather than running away from their problems, facing them and even enduring a bit of pain is the way to solving them. When they do follow the path of growth, they can be even more inspiring and enthusiastic.

Sevens need to learn to live in the present—to be aware of what is happening right now instead of always looking to the next thing and missing what's in the present. They get their joy from the anticipation of what is in their future and lose out on the current joy.

If you are a Seven and experience a negative emotion or uncomfortable situation, pause before jumping to the next thing. Let yourself feel the emotion or analyze the situation instead of quickly moving on. Think about why you are trying to avoid it and determine what you can learn through it.

Try to focus on others, be a servant, and find out what other people's needs are. Instead of always trying to lighten the mood or pointing out all the positives, take a minute to think about the negatives. Some people may be suffering around you. If you continue to try to lighten the mood instead of listening and helping them through their hurt, they might become resentful and pull away from you. To help you in these growth steps, here are some of the spiritual disciplines you may want to focus on.

THE SPIRITUAL DISCIPLINES FOR SEVENS

The spiritual disciplines that may come naturally for Sevens are worship and service. Sevens feel alive when they are engaging in music and praise. It's an outward expression of the joy they have in their hearts. When they worship, especially with a group, they are encouraged and lifted. The challenge in worship is that they don't just enjoy focusing on who God is and what he's done for them, but use it as an escape.

Service is enjoyable to Sevens. Helping others and finding joy in making someone else's life easier, to uplift the people around them, is natural to them. They like to be around people, so when service can be part of a group or community, Sevens thrive. Their motivation is usually not to be seen by others, which can be a problem for other numbers, but they enjoy being with and living life with other people. Acts of service fulfill not only the need to help and give back but also being part of a community and receiving the joy and contentment they long for.

Solitude and silence may be more difficult for Sevens. Sitting with and listening to God allows them the freedom to step out of performance mode—putting on the optimistic front and turning everything into a positive side—and face their disappointments and fears. They can enjoy communion with God, which serves as a reminder that their identity and worth are not based on how they feel or how others feel about them, but on God's love for them and who they are in Christ.

Fasting may be difficult for Sevens. It strips them from the addiction to experiences and busyness and denies the adrenaline rush. Fasting reminds them that God's love and true joy don't depend on circumstances or experiences but the person of Jesus Christ. It takes away the addicted, overly dependent nature and awakens their true hunger for the presence of God. God has put a hunger inside all of us for him, but Sevens can confuse that with experience, fun, and excitement. When they strip that away, it helps them understand that Christ is the center, and Christ wants to fill the missing part of who they are.

The key verse for the Seven is John 4:14: "But whoever drinks of the water that I will give him will never be thirsty again. The water that I will give him will become in him a spring of water welling up to eternal life" (ESV). The key thought to remember is, *The essence of the abundant, joyful life is in Christ. He wants my joy to be complete in him, not in adrenaline or experiences.*

One of the many great aspects of the Seven is that they let people see the joy of the Lord when they are serving God in a healthy way. The world needs you. You have a way of inspiring and encouraging us. You take the boring routine out of our lives.

QUESTIONS FOR A SEVEN

1. How do I take time to enjoy what is currently happening in my life?

2. How am I willing to accept that life isn't always fun and exciting?

3. When do I observe others to see what their needs are?

4. In what situations do I make impulsive decisions?

5. How can I take time to listen to and understand those I am in relationship with?

6. When am I willing to work through emotions of anger, pain, and fear?

QUESTIONS FOR THOSE WHO WORK OR LIVE WITH A SEVEN

1. How can I listen to their ideas and encourage them to share what they are thinking?

2. When am I willing to have casual conversations with them, not always trying to be serious?

3. How can I encourage them to share what they are feeling and help them find ways to work through their emotions?

4. How can I remain upbeat and positive when giving feedback or constructive criticism?

VERSES FOR MEDITATION FOR SEVENS

Give praise to the Lord, proclaim his name; make known among the nations what he has done. Sing to him, sing praise to him; tell of all his wonderful acts. Glory in his holy name; let the hearts of those who seek the Lord rejoice.

1 Chronicles 16:8–10

• • • • •

Nehemiah said, "Go and enjoy choice food and sweet drinks, and send some to those who have nothing prepared. This day is holy to our Lord. Do not grieve, for the joy of the Lord is your strength."

Nehemiah 8:10

. . . . .

Take delight in the Lord, and he will give you the desires of your heart.

Psalm 37:4

. . . . .

Praise the Lord. Blessed are those who fear the Lord, who find great delight in his commands.

Psalm 112:1

. . . . .

"For I know the plans I have for you," declares the Lord, "plans to prosper you and not to harm you, plans to give you hope and a future."

Jeremiah 29:11

. . . . .

Then he said to them all: "Whoever wants to be my disciple must deny themselves and take up their cross daily and follow me. For whoever wants to save their life will lose it, but whoever loses their life for me will save it. What good is it for someone to gain the whole world, and yet lose or forfeit their very self? Whoever is ashamed

of me and my words, the Son of Man will be ashamed
of them when he comes in his glory and in the glory
of the Father and of the holy angels."

Luke 9:23–26

. . . . .

But whoever drinks the water I give them will never
thirst. Indeed, the water I give them will become in
them a spring of water welling up to eternal life.

John 4:14

. . . . .

Rather, he made himself nothing by taking the very
nature of a servant, being made in human likeness.

Philippians 2:7

. . . . .

Rejoice in the Lord always. I will say it again: Rejoice!
Let your gentleness be evident to all. The Lord is near.

Philippians 4:4–5

. . . . .

TYPE EIGHT

THE CHALLENGER

Fear: Being or appearing weak

Verse to Memorize: But he said to me, 'My grace is sufficient for you, for my power is made perfect in weakness.' Therefore I will boast all the more gladly of my weaknesses, so that the power of Christ may rest upon me. (2 Cor. 12:9 ESV)

TYPE EIGHT OVERVIEW

The next number in the Body (Instinctual) triad, with the Nine and One, is the Eight, known as the Challenger. Their passion is lust, which, for them, is the lust for power. Eights can be confrontational and aggressive. People often feel dominated and controlled by them, but the Eight may not see this or understand why. They are surprised when others say they are intimidating. They see the world in black and white; something is either right or wrong, true or false, friend or enemy. They are not afraid of a disagreement and usually enjoy a good debate. When they are healthy and strong in their Christian walk, God uses them to serve the weak and marginalized in our society. Their personalities aid them in making differences, such as taking bold stands against injustice.

Eights' basic fear is being harmed or controlled by others; therefore, their basic desire is to protect themselves and to make sure they are in control. They use their instincts to decide who is and is not safe. "Can I trust this person? If so, what can I trust them with?" They do not express soft emotions, such as sadness or hopelessness, because they don't want their emotions to be used against them. Sometimes those emotions make them feel out of control. Anger feels safer, because they do not need to let their guard down to express it. They can appear to be insensitive, because they distance themselves from feeling hurt, weak, or fearful, as well as stepping back from people who show these emotions.

Eights seek to find the most direct route to get what they need or what. They are intense, energetic, honest, straightforward, fun, and generous. They are hard workers and take on the role of protector for the persecuted or marginalized. They react physically to unfairness; it feels like a punch in the gut. They don't want to see themselves as being vulnerable, so they help others who are.

For Eights, anger is an underlying emotion that comes out only when the Eight is pushed emotionally or physically or when their authority is questioned. However, most Eights' anger flares and subsides quickly, and they never feel regret or guilt over letting it out—what's done is done. They have released that emotion and moved on. However, they may leave others in wake of their anger, not realizing people are still processing what happened. They are not afraid of conflict and are willing to confront others. In fact, they usually use confrontation as a way to test if someone will stand up for themselves or remain loyal to their values. They want people to stand up to them and be strong. Doing so earns an Eight's respect.

They do not like to submit to authority; however, their attitude is not pure rebellion. It's because they believe the rules are wrong, while the Eights' rules are right. When Eights walk into a room, people know that someone in authority has entered. They have a confident air about them, taking control of a situation if there is a lack of leadership or lack of effective leadership. However, Eights respect effective leaders. They desire independence and to be in control of their lives. They are blind to their weaknesses and challenges.

THE THREE SUBTYPES OF EIGHTS

Like every other type, Eights can be understood as one of three subtypes.

The Self-Preservation Eight
The self-preservation Eight's goal is to pursue everything needed to survive, including going against social norms.

They feel attacked if someone challenges their thoughts or beliefs. They are not worried about what other people think of them or what the social norms are. They may feel that if a person isn't willing to get to know and understand them, it doesn't matter what they think. They hide their feelings more than the other Eights and are terse and direct with others. They are good at bartering and bargaining, so they negotiate deals extremely well. They seek revenge for injustice, but they don't always understand why. It is a subconscious response.

The Social Eight

This is the counter type for the Eight. They are more mellow, fun, and outgoing. They find social justice causes to work with and strive to protect others. They are loyal to those they protect and will fight to the end to make things right for them. They are not always willing to follow the social norms to protect their causes. They are sensitive to people, more so than the other types of Eights. They do not like to work individually, so they look for causes to be involved in a group.

This Eight uses their intellect the most; they are willing to think through a situation. In most cultures, the female Eight is perceived quite differently from the male Eight. In some cases, the woman may be considered overbearing (negative perception) while the man may be looked at as a leader (positive perception). This is changing in our current world, but for the older female Eights, it was probably difficult to have these personality traits.

The Sexual Eight

The sexual Eight is the most rebellious of the Eights' subtypes. They do not like rules and usually have trouble working on a team. They can appear antisocial, because they are more selective about whom they choose to be with. They are the most emotional of the Eights, being in tune with their emotions and willing to acknowledge them. They take pride in not following social norms and are the most likely to take over a situation when they walk into it. They are charismatic and, as the psychologist Naranjo says, "They have more colors in their feathers."[5] They stand out and are proud of it. They can be possessive and controlling in relationships; therefore, they have difficulty developing intimacy.

WHAT EIGHTS FEAR MOST

The Eight fears being out of control, being controlled by others, and being hurt by others. They stand up for themselves and strive to avoid relationships or situations that could jeopardize their control. Much of their time is spent trying to keep control when living out their Christian faith, thus struggling with letting the Holy Spirit guide them. Giving their lives to someone else scares them. However, it is the journey that allows them to overcome their fears and find joy and peace in this world.

EIGHTS IN THE BIBLE

Samson was known for his strength. His presence was evident when he entered a room. But he misused that strength on many occasions. He had several instances of unhealthy anger and aggression, leaving behind a path of destruction. He wanted to be in control of situations, people, and relationships. His weakness was women. His vice of lust was not only for control but also a strong sexual desire. He had a hard time letting Delilah into his life, and when he did, she betrayed him.

Another biblical character that emanated the Eight's personality is John the Baptist. He was direct in his speech and not afraid to confront the spiritual leaders of his time. He did not care what others thought of him but strove to use his energy for justice and urged repentance to bring healing to his people. He used his intense drive for justice to advocate for the powerless and became a trailblazer for Christ to come in even more power.

GROWTH FOR EIGHTS

But the fruit of the Spirit is love, joy, peace, patience, kindness, goodness, faithfulness, gentleness, self-control; against such things there is no law.
(Gal. 5:22–23 ESV)

The fruit of the Spirit is where growth starts for every number. Eights naturally exhibit kindness to the underdog or those who are being treated unjustly. The Eights' growth comes through the discovery that the kindness of God goes out to even those who are against them. We can all get on board with being kind to people who deserve it. But the Holy Spirit gives us kindness toward those who don't deserve it. Consider these verses from Paul:

> If the part of the dough offered as firstfruits is holy, then the whole batch is holy; if the root is holy, so are the branches. If some of the branches have been broken off, and you, though a wild olive shoot, have been grafted in among the others and now share in the nourishing sap from the olive root, do not consider yourself to be superior to those other branches. If you do, consider this: You do not support the root, but the root supports you. You will say then, "Branches were broken off so that I could be grafted in. Granted. But they were broken off because of unbelief, and you stand by faith. Do not be arrogant, but tremble. For if God did not spare the natural branches, he will not spare you either. Consider therefore the kindness and sternness of God: sternness to those who fell, but kindness to you, provided that you continue in his kindness. Otherwise, you also will be cut off. And if they do not persist in unbelief, they will be grafted in, for God is able to graft them in again. (Rom. 11:16–23)

When we strive to be in control of everything, we leave God out of the leadership role he should have in our lives. Learning to let go and trust God and others with ideas, decisions, and direction can help the Eight's growth process. They need to be in close connection with people, which will, at times, require Eights to be vulnerable, even when hurting. Others know Eights are brave but need to see that Eights are brave enough to let people in. When they can begin to forgive others, it will open a whole new connection between the Eight and God. Admitting when they are wrong is another growth point for the Eights. Saying, "I'm sorry; I was wrong," is healthy. Life is so much better when we have relationships that are open and honest.

If you are an Eight, use your gifts to inspire others rather than asserting authority over them. Recognize when people pull away from you because you come across as intimidating. Seek to understand what about the conversation made you feel you had to become so big that it hurt someone else. Including others in the process of decision-making and moving a cause forward can be very rewarding.

Learn how to handle your anger. As an Eight, you feel intensely in your body, making it hard to be productive when in this state. Your anger usually revolves around injustice or protecting others, so channel that anger into productive action. Instead of revenge, think reform. To help you in these growth steps, here are some of the spiritual disciplines you may want to focus on.

THE SPIRITUAL DISCIPLINES FOR EIGHTS

As we look at spiritual disciplines for the Eight, service and worship may come easily. Eights are energized by opportunities to stand up for the marginalized. "To act justly and to love mercy" (Mic. 6:8) expresses how the Eights act out their faith. They are filled with compassion for the underdog and the hurting, so they like to get their hands dirty by righting wrongs. They get involved and stand in the shoes of those they are serving. They have a great capacity for empathy and compassion. Physically stepping in and taking a stand is rewarding. Acts of service help them put hands and feet to their faith.

Fasting can come naturally for the Eight because they feel like they are in control. It can give them a sense of being strong and powerful. They have the discipline to fast but need to be vulnerable to the fasting experience in a different way: Let go of the control and allow the presence of God to take over.

The disciplines of confession and prayer can be a struggle for Eights. Both require a sense of vulnerability. Confession involves opening up and being honest about weaknesses and temptations. Eights need accountability from people they can trust, thus they don't have to hide behind the facade of strength and power. They do well to embrace that in their weaknesses Christ's strength will prove to be enough.

Prayer requires them to lay down their pride and turn to God for his leading. Giving up the idea that they can control everything and allowing the power of God to work through them is a struggle. Accepting the attributes of God will help them to release their hold on life and rely on God to lead and guide them. Praying for others is easier than acknowledging their own needs and desires. Speaking the truth to God, even when they know he knows, leaves an Eight feeling vulnerable and weak.

The key verse for an Eight is, "But he said to me, 'My grace is sufficient for you, for my power is made perfect in weakness.' Therefore I will boast all the more gladly about my weaknesses, so that Christ's power may rest on me. That is why, for Christ's sake, I delight in weaknesses, in insults, in hardships, in persecutions, in difficulties. For when I am weak, then I am strong" (2 Cor. 12:9–10). The key thought for the Eight is, *I will allow my weakness to keep me humble and rely on God's strength, grace, and power to keep moving me closer to being who he wants me to be.*

The world needs Eights to shake things up. We need you to get things done. Someone needs to rock the boat and do the Lord's work. Continue to be the strong advocate for the weak, but be sure to bring those of us with compassion and grace along with you. You are a natural leader and look for ways to take care of the underdogs in our society. When you allow God to use that drive for his purposes, you will find fulfillment, joy, and contentment while changing the world.

QUESTIONS FOR AN EIGHT

1. Do I take time to listen to others' ideas?

2. Can I discern when to step back and let someone else lead?

3. Have I surrendered every area of my life to the Lord, or am I holding on to control in one or more areas?

4. Am I able to be vulnerable with my partner?

5. Am I aware that others may find me intimidating or overpowering?

6. Can I pause to think through a response, or do I react without thinking?

QUESTIONS FOR THOSE WHO WORK OR LIVE WITH AN EIGHT

1. Do I allow the Eight to share new ideas and listen to their strategies?

2. Do I avoid small talk? How can I make practical, logical suggestions.

3. Do I give feedback with respect?

4. Do I let them know when they are taking over a situation?

5. Do I stand up for my values and ideas with the Eight?

VERSES FOR MEDITATION FOR EIGHTS

It is God who arms me with strength
and keeps my way secure.
Psalm 18:32

. . . . .

The LORD makes firm the steps of the one who
delights in him; though he may stumble, he will not fall,
for the LORD upholds him with his hand.
Psalm 37:23–24

. . . . .

Love does not delight in evil but rejoices with the
truth. It always protects, always trusts,
always hopes, always perseveres.
1 Corinthians 13:6–7

. . . . .

Therefore, since we have such
a hope, we are very bold.
2 Corinthians 3:12

. . . . .

Therefore we are always confident and know that as long
as we are at home in the body we are away from the
Lord. For we live by faith, not by sight. We are confident,
I say, and would prefer to be away from the body and
at home with the Lord. So we make it our goal to please
him, whether we are at home in the body or away from it.

2 Corinthians 5:6–9

*　*　*　*　*

TYPE NINE

THE PEACEMAKER

Fear: Fear of loss or separation

Verse to Memorize: God the Father knew you and chose you long ago, and his Spirit has made you holy. As a result, you have obeyed him and have been cleansed by the blood of Jesus Christ. May God give you more and more grace and peace. (1 Peter 1:2 NLT)

TYPE NINE OVERVIEW

The last number in the Body (instinct) triad, with the Eight and One, is the Nine, also known as the Peacemaker. For Nines, life is all about bringing people together and being at peace with others and themselves. They tend to go with the flow and avoid conflict of any kind.

Nines' passion is sloth—not physical laziness, but emotional and relational laziness. This does not mean that Nines are not active or hard workers. This laziness pertains to their self-care or self-awareness. They live for other people. Their internal laziness is in knowing who they are, what they stand for, and what they like and dislike. Therefore, they can lack passion and fire, even losing their creativity and imagination, because they stop looking into their inner selves.

Nines desire to maintain the status quo and keep the peace. They want their everyday lives to run smoothly. They put the betterment of the collective over an individual, measuring the whole group to perceive the emotions at work and then figuring out how to make peace with everybody. They are adaptable, likable, and good at defusing conflict. They make people feel included and respected, but Nines can be complacent. They do not like to be the center of attention, preferring to remain in the background and in their comfort zones.

Nines struggle with procrastination and indecision. It is very hard for them to make decisions based on what they want, because what's best for the collective gets in the way. They can be stubborn and irritable when doing something they don't like. This can happen quite often, because they go along with the collective, not choosing to do what they enjoy.

The Nine's core emotion is anger, but they tend to avoid anger because they don't like to feel it. They usually become passive-aggressive with their anger, trying not to show their emotion but wanting to change the situation. Anger, in their minds, causes conflict, so it is to be avoided. They may get to a point where they erupt, but they typically express anger with passive-aggressive behavior. They want to get their point across in a nonconfrontational way.

Because they are in the middle of the Body triad, Nines suppress their bodies. They can "go to sleep" to their bodies, which means they are self-forgetting. They have a hard time articulating their needs or wants. They struggle with following their intuition and being bold and courageous.

The strength of the Nine is their ability to intuitively sense how to resolve conflict. They can see problems from the perspective of all the types and how to repair relationships and conflict. They make excellent mediators because they see all sides of an issue. But they have to be willing to courageously share what needs to happen in the mediation process.

THE THREE SUBTYPES OF NINES

As with all the other types, Nines have three subtypes.

The Self-Preservation Nine

The self-preservation Nine is more about physical comforts than the other subtypes of Nine. They find comfort in the world by satisfying their physical needs. Activities such as eating, sleeping, and reading fulfill that need, as well as any physical work they enjoy. This Nine is focused on routine. They like the familiar and repetitive. They don't like change or relate much to abstractions. They prefer to be alone.

The self-preservation Nine can look like a One or an Eight, which may seem strange, but it is because they can be very stubborn and irritable and have a strong presence about them. However, they handle their emotions differently. I was listening to a podcast panel of Nines, and one of the participants, talking about being frustrated with someone, said, "I was so mad that I needed to take a nap." If you can relate, you are probably a Nine.

The Social Nine

This Nine is about group focus. This is the counter type because we don't usually think of Nines as being social. They usually like to be by themselves, but the social Nine integrates with groups. They long to feel like they're part of something because they tend to feel like they don't belong anywhere. This is a lot like a Four, but Nines don't deal with emotions as a Four does. They work extra hard at fitting into a group to appear outgoing and energetic. They can be extroverted because they need that acceptance within the group. This Nine feels as if they are not loved, and so they seek it within that group.

The Sexual Nine

The sexual Nine is more about an individual focus, fusing with, or becoming more like another individual. Usually, fusing is a subconscious action. Nines tend to feel lonely and abandoned. To fill that emptiness, they unite with another person, connecting so closely with the other person that all of their likes match the other person's. Because of this fusion, they have great difficulty standing up for what their values are if they differ from this person's. They often don't realize what their subconscious is doing, but they give in to the other person's wants and desires. They are uncertain about their identities, and they lack structure. They can be so focused on meeting the other person's needs that they betray their own. They may become passive-aggressive as they realize that this isn't who they are, yet not understanding why they've allowed themselves to get so far into being like the other person.

WHAT NINES FEAR MOST

The Nine's greatest fear is loss or separation. They don't want to be separated from either the group or the person they're strongly connected to. In many cases, as the Nines were growing up, they were not heard. Either their opinions were overridden by a forceful parent or sibling, or they were so easygoing that their opinions were not even considered. A Nine has a hard time putting into words their wants and needs and can justify not getting what they want because it makes a situation easier. To avoid conflict, they tend to put their feelings and values on the back burner when other people have strong opinions. When feeling frustrated or angry, they distract themselves so as not to be uncomfortable within themselves.

Although they can often see how to solve a problem and are able to empathize with others easily, their desire to avoid conflict causes them to hold their thoughts and ideas for resolution to themselves. Their fear of loss of relationship is greater than their desire to make the relationship stronger.

NINES IN THE BIBLE

Abraham seemed to go with the flow of God's plan, or else he tried to mediate between others and God. He tried to avoid conflict when he told his wife to say she was his sister (Gen. 12:10–20). Oftentimes, when trying to avoid conflict, the Nine makes the situation worse, as we saw in Abraham's situation with the pharaoh. He strived to be at peace with those around him, for example, by allowing Lot to choose from the flock first when they separated. When God told Abraham his plan for Sodom and Gomorrah, Abraham became a mediator. He thought he saw something good in the cities that should be saved. Abraham seems to have several of the characteristics of the Nine, but we can never know what motivates someone, so these examples are based on outward appearances.

GROWTH FOR NINES

But the fruit of the Spirit is love, joy, peace, patience,
kindness, goodness, faithfulness, gentleness,
self-control; against such things there is no law.
(Gal. 5:22–23 ESV)

The fruit of the Spirit is where growth starts for every number. Nines tend to crave and create peace in everyday life. As the power of the Spirit works in their lives, they hold on to the peace that the world cannot take away. "Peace I leave with you; my peace I give you. I do not give to you as the world gives. Do not let your hearts be troubled and do not be afraid" (John 14:27).

As the Nine strives to create peace around them, they minimize the problem or conflict. Usually, they do this to avoid conflict or unpleasantness. They need to recognize when they are letting others take charge or run over them. They can discover how to directly address an unpleasant situation by watching how others do it.

If you are a Nine, observe someone who is handling conflict in a healthy way and watch how they address it. Ignoring or becoming apathetic to the problem will usually result in passive-aggressive behavior toward the individuals involved. Accept that conflict is a part of life and that working through conflict can be a good thing. As a Nine, you have the ability to see the world through other types' lenses. So, use that gift, along with the Holy Spirit's guidance, to share what you notice about the conflict from your view, as well as from the other person's view. Let them know that you can see their point, but show how their viewpoint can be part of the conflict. This can be challenging, but the power of the Holy Spirit allows us to speak the truth in love and share the knowledge we have with others to contribute to the kingdom of God.

Because Nines avoid listening to their bodies, it's good to find a physical activity you can regularly participate in and connect with your body. Joining a gym, walking group, or other community physical activity will allow you not only to connect with your body but build relationships in a non-threatening environment.

Finally, facing the "negative" emotions Nines feel will help them grow. Everyone feels anger, sadness, hurt, and frustration, and understanding that they can have and express these emotions in a healthy way will move them through the peacemaking process more easily. When we suppress these emotions, they fester and cause us to pull away from others. Take time, maybe on a nature walk, to let yourself experience these emotions that you are holding on to. Be willing to walk outside and scream once in a while, letting out the emotion that has built up. Also, take time to allow the Holy Spirit to lead you to the things you have buried and begin to heal those hurts. To help you in these growth steps here are some of the spiritual disciplines you may want to focus on.

THE SPIRITUAL DISCIPLINES
FOR NINES

Solitude and silence can come easily for Nines. The discipline of retreating with God comes easiest through being in nature. Nature tends to bring peace and order to their world. It reminds them that their Creator is in control. They also like to be alone and retreat into a world of quiet and solitude when the chaotic world seems to be closing in. However, the Nine needs to be careful that the retreat does not keep them from their emotional needs and those of others. They tend to lose themselves and withdraw from the world.

Study and prayer can be more challenging for Nines. Studying the Word of God and being diligent in it can help the Nine recenter and remember that we serve a God of peace. Our God is in control, and he is where their peace is— not in circumstances and people. Nines need to study the truth and gain the courage to share that truth with others, understanding that declaring truth is a loving thing to do.

Prayer can also be challenging for the Nine, because it reconnects them with their emotional side. Opening up to God about their struggles and needs helps them recenter around the presence of Christ. It can also revive the most important relationship: their relationship with Christ. Prayer can give the Nine the passion and courage needed to step out in faith and be heard.

A key verse for the Nine is Ephesians 4:15: "Instead, speaking the truth in love, we will grow to become in every respect the mature body of him who is the head, that is, Christ." The key thought for the Nine to remember is, *Speaking the truth in love is what is asked of me. Be willing to be bold and give an objective voice to what is happening around me. My peace comes from Christ, not from circumstances.*

QUESTIONS FOR A NINE

1. When am I willing to be open and honest about my needs with those closest to me?

2. How do I hold on to my anger and let it build? Do I notice when I am being passive-aggressive with those around me?

3. When do I enjoy bringing others together and helping to mediate conflict?

4. Am I willing to be outspoken when I see what would bring peace to a situation?

QUESTIONS FOR THOSE WHO WORK OR LIVE WITH A NINE

1. How can I create an environment in which the Nine feels safe stating their needs or wants?

2. When do I encourage them to share their feelings or opinions?

3. When do I allow room for small talk in a conversation and let them share what is happening in their life?

4. How can I remain calm and patient when trying to resolve a conflict with them?

VERSES FOR MEDITATION FOR NINES

My heart is not proud, Lord, my eyes are not haughty;
I do not concern myself with great matters or things too
wonderful for me. But I have calmed and quieted
myself, I am like a weaned child with its mother; like
a weaned child I am content. Israel, put your hope in
the Lord both now and forevermore.

Psalm 131

* * * * *

Look at the birds of the air; they do not sow or reap or
store away in barns, and yet your heavenly Father feeds
them. Are you not much more valuable than they?

Matthew 6:26

* * * * *

For we are God's handiwork, created in Christ Jesus to do
good works, which God prepared in advance for us to do.

Ephesians 2:10

* * * * *

For this reason I kneel before the Father, from whom every
family in heaven and on earth derives its name. I pray
that out of his glorious riches he may strengthen you with
power through his Spirit in your inner being, so that Christ

may dwell in your hearts through faith. And I pray that you, being rooted and established in love, may have power, together with all the Lord's holy people, to grasp how wide and long and high and deep is the love of Christ, and to know this love that surpasses knowledge—that you may be filled to the measure of all the fullness of God. Now to him who is able to do immeasurably more than all we ask or imagine, according to his power that is at work within us, to him be glory in the church and in Christ Jesus throughout all generations, for ever and ever! Amen.

Ephesians 3:14–21

* * * * *

For this reason I remind you to fan into flame the gift of God, which is in you through the laying on of my hands.

2 Timothy 1:6

* * * * *

Who have been chosen according to the foreknowledge of God the Father, through the sanctifying work of the Spirit, to be obedient to Jesus Christ and sprinkled with his blood: Grace and peace be yours in abundance.

1 Peter 1:2

* * * * *

GUIDELINES
FOR
FASTING

1. Learn from an experienced teacher. If you have little or no practice with fasting in the Wesleyan way, seek the guidance of a spiritual director, pastor, or Christian friend skilled in fasting.

2. Prepare physically for the fast. If you are taking any medication, consult with your physician to choose a fast that does not conflict with your daily health practices.

3. Prepare spiritually for the fast. Ask the Holy Spirit to guide you, and listen to his response. Do not get so focused on the act of fasting that you forget the purpose of fasting— to shift attention from earthly things to spiritual things. You are going to meet God.

4. Prepare nutritionally for the fast. Decide whether you're going to do a complete fast (water only), a no-solid-food fast (allows milk, juice, coffee, and tea), a no-meat fast,

or some other fast. There are no fixed rules. Simply prepare yourself to meet God. Keep it simple, and keep the fast you set out to do. Some forms of fasting are more difficult than others. In time, the Spirit will lead you to try different types of fasts.

5. Determine the length of your fast. Start small, and then as you feel moved to do so, you can do longer fasting practices.

6. Stay hydrated. Drink plenty of water while fasting, no matter what kind of fast you choose.

7. Be mindful of your health. Fasting for multiple days is more complex than a twenty-four-hour fast. Make certain your doctor is aware of your intention for a longer fast and that you have agreed on a plan that is not harmful to your health.

8. Make God the sole focus of your fast. Do not use fasting as a means to gain the attention or admiration of others (see Matthew 6:16–18).

9. Expect something supernatural and spiritual to happen. Jesus fasted for forty days before he began his earthly ministry. He fasted and prayed all night before he called the twelve disciples to follow him more closely. Some miracles of spiritual deliverance came about only by prayer and fasting. As you follow Jesus' teaching and example in faith and obedience, expect something to happen.

For more study on the subject, read John Wesley's sermon on Matthew 6:16–18, the seventh discourse in the series "Upon Our Lord's Sermon on the Mount" (1747). It contains an extended discussion of the spiritual benefits of fasting. Find it here: http://www.wbbm.org/john-wesley-sermons/serm-027.htm.

MEDITATION, STUDY, SOLITUDE, SILENCE

MEDITATE

1. Find a passage of Scripture that resonates with you.

2. Write it down on an index card.

3. Read it slowly several times.

4. Write down what it means to you both spiritually and practically.

5. Think about it and meditate on the passage throughout the day.

MEDITATE/STUDY

1. Meditate on a section of Scripture. As questions and other verses come to mind, use page 153 to write them down and then return to the section you were focused on.

2. After the meditation time, study the questions and other verses that came to mind to see what else God wants to teach you through that selection.

STUDY

You can use an online Bible to look at Scripture in a new way.

1. Read the verses in other versions.

2. Look up Hebrew or Greek meanings of words that stand out to you.

3. Read a commentator's view of the section you are studying.

4. Look at maps when the selection talks about a place.

5. Study the Jewish culture to understand their customs and traditions.

SOLITUDE/SILENCE

1. Set aside thirty to sixty minutes to be with God.

2. Select soft music, nature sounds, or silence.

3. Create a comfortable spot where you can sit or lie down.

4. Allow the Holy Spirit to speak to you. Listen and relax.

MEDITATION SHEET

This is the sheet I use for my meditation time. Feel free to copy it, or you can use a notebook and create these sections on a blank sheet of paper. Use whatever helps you keep your focus on the Scripture.

DATE	SCRIPTURE VERSE/PHRASE ADDRESS	OTHER BIBLE VERSE THAT COMES TO MIND

FREEFORM MEDITATION	
	RESEARCH I WANT TO FOLLOW UP WITH
	TO DO LIST

PRAYER JOURNAL

This is a sample of my prayer journal page. Feel free to copy it or use a notebook or create these sections on a blank sheet of paper. It is amazing to see God's hand at work in the world around us when we write down our requests and praises.

Date

Adoration

People I said I would pray for

Praise

Requests

NOTES

Introduction

1. Charles W. Carter, R. Duane Thompson, and Charles R. Wilson, eds., *A Contemporary Wesleyan Theology*, vol. 2 (Grand Rapids, MI: Zondervan, 1983), 885.

2. Mildred Bangs Wynkoop, *A Theology of Love* (Kansas City, MO: Beacon Hill, 1972), 201.

3. A. W. Tozer and Marilynne E. Foster, *Tozer on the Holy Spirit: A 365-Day Devotional* (Chicago: Moody, 2020), 296.

4. "Enneagram Personality Type Indicator," Safe Harbor Christian Counseling, http://www.safeharbor1.com/documents/Enneagram-Personality-Type-Indicator.pdf, accessed July 14, 2022.

Type Eight—The Challenger

1. Beatrice Chestnut, *The Complete Enneagram: 27 Paths to Greater Self-Knowledge*, read by Randye Kaye (Old Saybrook, CT: Tantor Audio, 2018). Audible audio ed., 21 hr., 23 min.

ABOUT THE AUTHOR

Beverly and her husband married in 1989; they have been in ministry thirty of those years. She has a bachelor of science degree in secondary mathematics education from Oklahoma Wesleyan University and, at the time of this writing, is working on a master's in trauma and resiliency at Spring Arbor University. Beverly serves as a certified teacher in Michigan in an Alternative Education program. She and her husband have four amazing children—each one born in a different state—three awesome daughters-in-law, one outstanding son-in-law, and seven amazing grandkids.

Beverly has held many jobs over the years as a pastor's wife and God has used them all to shape who she is today: teacher, store clerk, office manager, librarian, stay-at-home and homeschool mom, business owner, speaker, and writer. God has used her in each position, and Beverly knows each job was placed in her life at the right time.

Beverly has studied the Enneagram for over five years and held workshops and online classes to teach others on the subject. It has changed the way she has viewed the world around her and taught her more about God's will for her life. She has been able to see her motivations more clearly and been given words to express her feelings and thought processes. It is one of many tools God has used to bring about spiritual growth. It is not the end-all and be-all tool, but it is one that has had an incredible impact on her personal life. Beverly hopes it helps you to grow as well.

For fun, Beverly likes camping, kayaking, playing tennis, bike riding, playing Pokémon Go and Animal Crossing, singing, scrapbooking, reading, writing, and loving on her family. She is truly blessed by God and hopes to continue on his mission for the rest of her life.